AN ESSENCE OF COOL

AN UNAUTHORIZED TRIBUTE TO MY BELOVED
MUSIC HERO GLENN FREY AND HIS BAND

*To Taylor Marie, Deacon, & Otis Frey, Glenn's children;
his greatest, proudest, most profound accomplishment of life.
The supreme part of him, blood of his blood. They represent a
celebration of his love, his legacy, and his memory.*

*And, for every fan that cherished the
miraculous gift of our dear Glenn Frey*

Painting by Anita G. Shepard

"Life is so ironic.
It takes sadness to know happiness,
noise to appreciate silence,
and absence to value presence."

~ Unknown

TABLE OF CONTENTS

PROLOGUE

"Just like rapids in the river or waves of the ocean that roll, then they go;
deep perpetual challenges will always come, and they will as well move on too.
We must accept the challenges just like we enjoy the whitecaps
and learn to roll with them both when we must."
~ (Unknown)

Where do I start, well on the first page.
But what do I note, words that engage.
Where to begin, with a story to unfold.
But why do I need, other books are told.
Where will it occur, where you impart.
But how do you state, a storybook start.

One simple head lift was all it took. *And here, is when it all started.* One lift and I moved forward to a lifelong passion.

If you have a passion, don't be mediocre about it. Give it your all. Don't just dip your toe in the water; jump into the deep end, submerging yourself headfirst. Push up forcefully, apply yourself, keep moving swiftly, steady forward strokes. Stroke, stroke, stroke...

When it came to Glenn Frey, that was 'The Anita Doctrine' that I believed in applying. Glenn Frey, his persona, his solo music, his thrilling talents and Eagle's music were a motivational set of factors that sweep me headfirst and kept me above water for 42 years.

I'm not saying it was tranquil waters every day. Naturally, there were moments and memories of when the river roared, raged, shifted and the creek-beds were rising. But would it be an exhilarating adventure without the rapids, the rowing, the drifting, the currents, the breathtaking scenes and the effort to reach the bank and that ultimate peaceful, easy calm.

Don't get me wrong, of course I didn't live, swim, float, and breathe Glenn Frey minute by minute. Life happens. We're way to busy living own life. Yet, strangely, it's almost like GF was infused into some part of my blood flow.

Glenn's bold majestic eagle spirit blew wind underneath my youthful wings. His music led me to believe I could fly high, soar above the clouds; gave joy in sunshine, determination to face storms, and strength to bear, cope, and survive any ominous crash landing.

And naturally, I know that Glenn was way, way more than 'just' a musician, that was only one element. There has always been that (teensy?) part of the band, yet each of us are multi-layered like an onion. As a musician, I am sure you must find that means to balance personal and professional aspects of life. Glenn seemed to have accomplished that well.

Further, many that knew or interacted with Glenn, on stage or off, describe him in the same manner: focused, disciplined, exciting, driven, energetic, perceptive, visional, direct, extremely talented, a decisive decision-maker, a teacher and one incredibly generous man.

But, like Glenn Frey said he was bitten by the little bug of rock 'n' roll maybe I was bitten by the Glenn bug, who knows. For me, Glenn was just Glenn, a cherished reward that vastly altered my life. Just an ordinary fan, that treasured the music of Glenn, Henley, the Eagles band. Their solo tunes as well were a dire life-ring that help me navigate through some good and some not as good times.

Smooth waters or rough, choppy gale forced hurricane, the Eagles and each stroke had a purpose. I know I cannot be alone in understanding what that music, these astonishing individuals, and the influence their spirit presented to our world.

I will be forever grateful for Glenn Frey, Henley, all the Eagles and what they gave in the form of their music to *my life*. It all started for me with just one simple tilted head lift. Who could ever have known that decades later the peace I was seeking and needed was granted with just a simple lowering head bow?

Had I come full circle?

SECTION ONE: GLENN

"In order to move on in our lives, sometimes we have to accept that we might never understand what has happened, some things are just meant to be..."
~ (Unknown)

Glenn Frey

Eagles Band Co-Founder

November 6, 1948-January 18, 2016

'Glenn Frey: Where are the words? Words. Right words? There are no words.'

Article Submitted Jan 19, 2016 Updated Jan 29, 2016

Publisher & Edited: The Courier Herald on Jan 27, 2016

The untimely passing of Glenn Frey announced on January 18, 2016 caught me off-guard. *"Everything...has been turned upside down, there's a cloud a fear and sorrow, an empty house, veil of tears, aches inside, try to be strong, there's a hole in the world tonight."* I am still struggling for words...it's beyond belief. Glenn is gone! Didn't flip on 'The Weather Channel' but immediately knew hell had actually frozen over.

Frey best known as Eagles band co-founder spun the music world into shock from this tragic news. Shattering words...unspoken words yearn to surface, profound sorrow, heartbroken devastation, cataclysmic upheaval. *"Your heart keeps saying it's just not fair. Something is wrong with this picture."* Our Glenn is gone. *"I will be with you everywhere you go. We've got to get over this somehow."* It's a stunning occurrence, utterly impossible to grasp. There are no right words that come to mind to sum these unsettling feelings- *"empty pages and a frozen pen"* yet of course Frey, Henley, those Eagles would have nailed it just right.

Maybe the right words are to simply say thank you Glenn. Thank you for sharing your soul-searching dreams; for the entertainment, education, *'elbow grease'*, the laughs, the return, the pursuit, the interesting appeal, your strength, infectious drive, and gifted accomplishments. We are forever grateful and blessed to have experienced this outstanding work, harmony, words, melody, your mind, fingers, precision, passion and ability.

In addition, thank you Eagles. Thank you so-so much for a masterful array of talent, your brilliant work, your refreshing magic, killer voices, that unyielding bravery, for an amazing journey and for simply being tremendous icons. Much appreciation for allowing the world to value your amazing legacy and for being the unshakeable profound rhythmic recordings to so many individuals' lives.

Like scores of struggling soul-searching teens during the mid to late 70's, Eagles rocked us right through high-school and beyond. Eagles' those faded jean-clad golden sun-drenched Pacific coast transplants singing blissful passionate natural-hallucinogenic paralyzing ballads. *"There's something you should know, we thank the stars above, out of the blue-across the dusty plains, out of the night you came along"* and suddenly changed lives. *"When we were hungry the music calls, it was in our blood, filled us up, bingeing' once you get a taste, held us close in our dreams."*

Pre-computer days of the Eighties were filled with radio, Billboard, MTV & VH1 music, and highlights. *"Sometime before the sun comes up"* there's a *radio out there that will "play that song."* As an Eagles fan you never forget those spellbinding songs, most of the words or the first time you laid eyes on that overwhelmingly distinct mellow-electrifying band. *"Like nothing I've ever known, they called it paradise"* it's was the beginning of a powerful life-altering event.

And you never forgot the spirited rock-star rebel one. Larger than life, the fearless sassy hard-hitting, bluesy-rock-N hipster; that Buttercup. "Brave as a Budweiser". That hair, those piercing eyes, those forceful methodical well-disciplined fingers-*'sparks fly from those fingertips'*. Fingertips on an electric in sculpted flared Levi's with legs that seemed to span from ceiling to floor, that hair, those wire-rimmed reflector shade sunglasses perched on top of that shimmering uninhibited head of hair, that golden 70's style droopy moustache, that magnificent black 'University of Colorado' Tee shirt. And, oh lord that non-*'raven hair-shining like the sun, sunlight in your hair'*, "Good evening we're the Eagles from Los Angeles" ripening into SoCal-southern country California rock. A soothing vocal tone with 'Take it Easy' then moving on to strumming a six-string flat top acoustic for an incredibly smoldering rendition of 'Lying Eyes'.

Ok, enough *"just had to set things right."* So, some teenage girls like hot superstar James Dean-Outlaw Country Desperado idols, probably the *"face in a crowd* the ones eating *lunch all by themselves. Caught up in the action, it's one fervent ride, people were smiling, we all belonged, and we all always wanted to play."* We were unconventional *"kinda bent, full of fun, out for a good time"* midnight flyN' 'Victims of Love'. *"We would sing clear and loud, you lift us up you made us strong, you made us tough, ain't no mountain, sugar, we can't climb."*

The attention of the words *"had a strong appeal, kept us alive* and committed *in a tame way. The times we spent, trying to reach the promised land, we thought we could change this world...just the way we planned. Tall drinks and drama. Standing against the world outside, waiting for the dust to settle down,* we *always wanted to stay another night.* 'Time passes things change' *some of our dreams came true-some of them stayed behind."* Then the *"years unfurl, seasons are slowly changing years go by...another year has come and gone, the years brought the railroad, those years keep rushing on"* and eventually those teens mature. 'In the Long Run' they slightly 'Get Over It', *"live from day to day-stop pretending you're somebody else"* and realize that while it's very nice that the Eagles are a sizzling handsome bunch of guys it's really all about that music, for the Eagles music stands the test of time.

Glenn and the Eagles seemed to always be moving, experimenting, examining, validating, trying things. The excitement of Eagles music pulsed through our thoughts, hearts, and seeped into our soul. *"It's in those moves; it pulses in your blood."* Frey declared the songs were "visual...pictures in your mind, the soundtracks to our lives." It was magical youthful moments, where we all connected and related to the songs. With impressive emotion, composition, allure and special creativity the band was able to rhythmically capture and impact practically every fiber, pattern, situation, or encounter we could experience all the while igniting an intoxicating combustible spark to the cultural beat of our lives.

No fillers Glenn Frey commented. No average music would do-which seemed top priority toward making every song outstanding in its own right. Glenn's stellar contribution to the music world, his incredible courage, his steely determination, and his fascinating career has been a rock-solid foundation for many.

From the beginning excitement of The Mushroom era, the Bob Seger days to playing a starring role as Ronstadt's backup cohort in 1971. Then, moving onward with Don Henley; each being natural born leaders and gifted musicians-to become legendary icons, pioneering their illustrative music style-formed Eagles band.

The exceptional union of Frey and Henley was a brilliant coupling, forming of a perfect union, a magnetic marital paring, a musical destiny created by the God's of harmony. Interwoven two of a kind, opposites-but possibly more alike than different; same goal, same dream, similar ideas.

William Shakespeare penned 'We are such stuff as dreams are made on' (The Tempest). It seemed obvious, the stuff their dreams were made on. Both were committed meticulous perfectionist. Glenn's precocious effortless creative talent and massive inspiration along with the collaborative mastermind focus of modest methodical low-key articulate music legend Don Henley the Eagles created some of the most beloved classic hit songs of our era.

As well, fellow band-members manifesting from Bernie Leadon, Randy Meisner, Timothy B Schmit, to Joe Walsh motivated the masses. Each one played their part with contoured pristine. Eagles manager Irving Azoff/Satan/Big Shorty-whose part and contributing factor should never be overlook or fact-finding mission of the right word, right image association as they were a regal bunch, distinct, warm-blooded, powerful sacred soaring and majestic! As a group they were historic songwriters and poignant vocalists, joining forces the flow of that captivating chart-topping music filled us, we thirstily drink it in. *"Only a passerby", but still we could "drink the wine from the winner's cup."*

"Running down the road" with our band we were also" trying to loosen my load" even when we had "a world of trouble on (the) mind." 'I Can't Tell You Why' but soaking Eagles, Frey, Henley's music in provides a serene source of *peaceful easy* survival, an internal release, a lyrical 'Soul-Searchin' escape. As

a unit, those perfectly pitched blended vocals, the organized words, the crafted instrumental sounds produce virtual expression that delivers an internal mental transformation. Not to underestimate the power of the lyrics, melody, sound, scales but possibly because the Eagles are champions of unmatched forthright rock harmony.

The gleeful piercing delivery for "Heartache Tonight", the liquid joy of "Take It Easy", rhythmic groove in "Tequila Sunrise", gentleness of "Saturday Night", mellow richness with "Waiting in the Weeds", divine soulfulness of "Peaceful Easy Feeling", classic "Desperado", captivating human destruction in "The Last Resort", vibrant lasting wisdom with "Part of Me", cautious acclaim to "Life in the Fast Lane"', deep fusion of "True Love", the heartfelt comfort for "You Are Not Alone", potential replacement roots with "New Kid", jazzy beat of "You Belong to the City", cool fire in "The Heat is On", clever seductive reality of "Lying Eyes", the assertive reach to "Take it to the Limit", gut-wrenching question "What do I do with my Heart?" and the curious inexplicable mystic maze (or more likely the potential dangers of addition, fame, yearning and excess) to "Hotel California". Yes, we all have our own thoughts on Hotel C. Henley did say that some things were just for them. Once again, he would be right.

"So often...we live our lives in chains" locked in deep never knowing it in *inside we hold our own key.* You always had the key; you knew just what to do with the words, tempo, pitch, cord, the tune. When done, it was blended sheer perfection: *"We could lose, **and** we could win...open up let's all climb in!"* Oh yeah, with your words you always took us on an incredible ride. A ride that like a musical quake was earth-moving and even from afar, climb in we did.

"Found the road to freedom, wild birds scattering the seeds...all you give is all you get, spiders spinning in the dark." Even during dark, spinning,

9

tumultuous times Frey, Eagles, the words, and the music were a constant comforting bright star. *"There are stars in every sky bright and glowing as you go."* A band that was always seeking, reaching for and finding the most harmonious stars, traveling with us all the way to Winslow AZ, *"we could see those stars but could we see the real light-just come on baby."*

But now, *"twist of fate...whatever time may take away, four men ride out... three ride back.* Is *it's time to leave behind some things from yesterday?"* This truly is the end of an era. One of those exceptionally rare national finales like Elvis, Ronnie Van Zant, John Lennon, Jerry Garcia, Glenn Frey. *"Is it all a game, where do you go after the party ends? There's nowhere else left to go."*

Eagles crafted mesmerizing songs that still after decades and decades touch way more lives than they may ever realize. Their extraordinary music played in the background fabric of our lives for over 4 decades. Forty years *"don't you know me after all these years?"*

It's an honor being a diehard Eagles fan. Unconditional honor. Eagles gave us so much, set standards, aspired to be pinnacles of success, insisted on specific regards to detail. They produced a fantastic timeless body of work. Will music ever sound the same? *"Somewhere out on that horizon, country garden in a shade, no more bridges burnin'."* The music that *'makes me wanta cry, feel it in my bones, the tide's eternal tune'* is sealed in recorded history. One song, one line, one word can trigger profound memories.

"Our lives have changed'; we see it slipping away, yet here on earth this old, old world just keeps turnin." Then, the world instantly stopped. *"The aftermath, the litter and the wreckage, right before our eyes a storm is coming. A stillness in the air, shadows lean heavy in the air, staring at the sea, sharks are lurking beneath."* I keep thinking wake-up, wake-up, wake-up; is this a virtual 1975 hallucination rebound, or in the band's historical documentary part

III please let there be an award-winning rewrite and studious editing for this unreal paradox. *"Standing at a crossroad, how did we get on this road? Time has brought us here to share these moments. There's no easy answer, words can break your heart. A bluebird with its heart removed. Holding back my tears. How long... will we weep? Feel so helpless, there must be something better. Oh my God, pain and sorrow, falling apart, looks like this is the end; don't say this is the end."*

On January 18th *"we heard it in the headlines. Turn on the tube; look at the news, there's trouble on the streets, all the news is bad. In the stillness I can hear a voice; something's come between us, a distant voice is calling me away. People in denial, there's a big train rolling, everything's exploded-crash. The world is torn and shaken,* turns *your heart into wood.* 'Ladies and Gentlemen... Elvis <u>has</u> truly left the building.' *Tell me you're not leaving, breaks your heart when someone leaves."*

"Most of Us Are Sad, Strange Weather, Cloudy Days". That was and will forever be a tragic date to any Eagles fan. *"The clouds roll-in, you could feel it, dark clouds in the sky,* a stormy day no rainbows, *a cold dark cloud, shadow rising on the darker side...night rolls in, blackness of an endless sky, the shadows come to stay...you could taste it."*

That day checked into rooms Hotel California wouldn't have opened. *"I think about you all through the day...remembering that amazing shadow of your smile. It's just like a dream, on a dark desert highway cool wind in my hair."* Clearly this nightmarish dream with just a few words has ripped us apart dropped us to our knees. *"Wearing me down, down on your knees...you can't find peace. It's a crime, doin' time in a lonesome prison. I'll be left behind."*

"It's so sad. Hide all the sadness you feel?" The sadness totally engulfs us. *"Muddy river runs so deep. Staring at the falling rain, rain keeps coming; river*

is rising, a river of darkness. We're washed away. Seems the whole wide world's gone crazy. You can't believe it's happening, it's such a bitter world."

There is no coming back from this moment. *"You won't be with me someday… that's how it's meant to be?"* Our poignant avalanche of tears flow. *"The time is coming-you don't know if you can explore the unknown. We don't know how to be alone. Only takes a breath or two to tear your world apart."* We say life is fragile, but most don't live or learn the wisdom of that lesson. *"I sit here wondering what we're really learnin'."* Learning? In a flickering moment the final chapter can be written. Glenn scripted the words of the first Eagles chapter and possibly the last.

"With all the stars to guide you, silent stars, still missing you." Glenn Lewis Frey will be terribly--terribly missed. *"Oh, they tell me there's a place over yonder."* In my humble opinion, Frey's absence place in the music world will be much in relation to a great soaring bird, a proud, unique symbol of class not just with a clipped, mangled or broken wing but in essence as if one wing has entirely vanished.

"Sometimes there's a part of me has to turn from here and go...it's those restless hearts that never mend." At this moment, everyone that *chased a dream, placed a bet,* admired, and loved Glenn Frey has a bleeding restless heart that is broken into shattered pieces. *"I'm getting old before my time; we're all running out of time...say goodbye to all this misery."* Personally, Glenn probably suffered way too often in a lot of severe pain, so if there is any consolation while our pain is vast, his pain is no more.

"Soul-searchin', not counting on tomorrow, we can never know about tomorrow, people don't run out of dreams." Glenn's dream, his legacy, mercifully his soundtracks of music will live on. *"Even with a shot of courage, marvel at why the right words never come."* Frey words might be wakeup-be strong, embrace life, appreciate the times shared; look forward to what is ahead-of course we will

never know but he would have expressed those words in a much more eloquent descriptive professional manner.

Glenn specified "every song should have a hero." Eagles' fans had found the hero. *"Be part of something good, leave something better behind."* Grief is varied and unpredictable. In the healing process, one realizes that a hero such as Glenn has fans that are a unique bonded family. Wish I understood why they, all of the Eagles, feel like members of our family when we know they are not? How can you let someone go that was like family and filled a delightful space of your life? How can a stranger-someone you don't even know be such a force in your life? How do you adapt to the emptiness?

"What's down the road beyond the hill, win or lose...until we find the bridge across forever...so many miles to go, until this grand illusion brings us home." In the aftermath of tragedy somehow, we painfully travel forward strong, aching, or weak. *Somehow, we'll survive;* we'll celebrate the life of Glenn Frey, the accomplishments he gave, and be forever grateful for those prized memories of our Eagle frozen in time.

"No more running...look at me-part of the lonely crowd-also running out of time." Watching through the years, early-on Frey appeared kinda shy, insecure, head-down, but still brave enough to take chances. Right before our eyes Eagles surfaced. Skills developed, confidence expanded, powerful words were penned, zestful energy built, belief soared, worldwide fan awareness occurred. Music improved, they grew and flew. Through their evolving dream and the power of Eagles music we believed we could change the world, but the world of the Eagles changed us. That dream, *that sentimental reason,* that chance Glenn Frey took, took charge, and changed our world.

Glenn Frey, the Eagle hero, the brave bud absolutely changed my world. His music, his words, his bravery, his journey *changed my life.* However, I never truly realized until this indescribable thunderbolt how deeply the Eagles world had influenced and continued to impact me for decades. The discovery of this band's music spun words into gold. They always made me wanna trek to Joshua Tree. Eagles may be just another band to some, and I do feel a little like that silly star-struck 14-year old-school girl, but it sure was fun.

Honestly, I know nothing about any of these guys, just expressing feelings from the heart of an outsiders seeking to look in, replay bittersweet memories, heal. In sharp contrast to any articulate Eagle, I am no writer, no gifted communicator just a blessed fan who struggles with what to think or say to avoid seeming freakishly bizarre.

Yet, while myself or other Eagles fans may struggle with timid words Don Henley wrapped it all up fashionably prior to the History of the Eagles Tour nailing it just right with the words: ***"this might be the last hooray for the Eagles... It's been an incredible experience for all of us, but it may be time to say adios and bow out gracefully."***

Regardless of this jolt, a fan's hurt could under no circumstances touch the tortured suffering of the family, friends, or loved ones. Sincere thoughts to Glenn's family-Cindy, Taylor, Deacon & Otis, the Eagles bandmates, Azoff, and the worldwide fan base who supported Eagles band.

"Staring' slowly cross the sky, it's so hard to say goodbye. Oh, and it's a hollow feelin'" when you realize we have to find the words to say our final goodbye. RIP Glenn, we love you dearly.

The Face that launched a thousand ships,
sang a million songs,
and broke a trillion hearts
Jan 18, 2016
~ Anita G Shepherd

SECTION TWO: GLENN LEWIS FREY

"The future has many names, for the weak it's unreachable, for the fearful it's unfamiliar, for the bold it's an opportunity."

~ (Unknown)

1: We Will Never Forget Glenn Frey

January 18, 2018: Year Two

The blessings you gave were too many to count
the ***hole*** you made is too large to fill
your presence your aura so eminent they chilled
as the stage show unfolds you built thrilling skill
but most of all with that music our spirits you lift
with the flick of a wrist the toss of that hair
for the reach of a cord the pluck of a riff string
the nod of your head in a group or alone
you made us believe we rode the ride along
'with ya' on the path of your
wide-searching earthly journey
giving treasures and memories to all with care
not just for Joe, Timmy, Henley, or Bern
but to and for all who came to arena or fair
a fearless force with magical fireworks of glare
you gave us your all and you gave us our share
what an incredibly enriching priceless gift
that was your task no more could we ask
except perhaps now you have comfort that last.

2: Addicted

November 2, 2015, Op-Ed

Hello, my name is Anita. I am a devoted loyal forty-plus years Eagles addict.

There are many diverse addictions, thankfully some are safe. Soaking music in live, to tape, vinyl, disc, app, revenue-based streaming, or whatever mean is of current popularity platform I stand firmly beside. The monkey was on my back-well essentially the eagles were in my windshield view and I didn't look back. I had that need-Eagles music fills, fuels, energies, satisfies... the desperate junkie.

Eagles music connects us to them-the guys, the songs, our needs our wants and always made me feel they understood. They gave us vision, the escape. We can see ourselves living out the words of their powerful moving songs. We recognize the emotion, we shared those same feelings in our days, our thrills, excursions, victories, vulnerabilities, relationships, sorrow, conquest, our regret, our heart, our past similar times, or situations.

That E music for fans, the common man, the silent majority, the enthralled audience, *"called it Paradise"* and know why. Our link those songs. Repetitive frequent pattern. Our uniting bond. A significant part of my personal habitual addition. The fix.

"Desperado", "Wasted Time", "Last Resort", "Lying Eyes", "Heartache", "New Kid", "Long Run", "Tequila Sunrise", "Take/Limit", "Try & Love A", "Get Over It", "BBF", "Hole/World", "PEF", "After the Thrill", "Take it Easy", "What do I do with..." as you know only a good ripple for their song bucket catalog. No mention of the heart-stopping dynamic solo works needed which was just as stunning.

Or later years the excitement of watching the ancient one with his young

16

son Deacon Frey side by side especially on, lord have mercy Nepotism Incorp at its best "*Werewolves of London*!" (Glenn and team 'werewolves' yet again playing ball and or music!)

Incidentally, striving to follow a dedication is a commitment for me only as one of admiration and yet one that remains far from the side of a stalker. Without crossing boundaries into lalaland as stalking is just too much work. Whose got time for that anyway and I'm just plain too lazy. Legally, and thankfully internet search engines research does not constitute stalking.

Assuredly, I am steadfast in my profound verbal confirmation of being a Glenn girl. But there are some who know me that disagree stating, "Glenn may have sucked you in, but you stayed because of Henhcn."

Now, if that were true the Glenn affect wouldn't have been such an adamant bonafied conviction. That voice, that talent, Mother of Joseph the hair, those aviator shades, that sweatband, the hair, and oh lord that black University of Colorado Tee shirt.

Somebody please, please, please tell me that tee has been preserved... And yes, I know everyone is so tired of me mentioning Glenn Frey hair, but I just can't seem to let it go as easily as he did...maybe that hair was a whole other narcotic...

On a different source, August 1, 2015 Don Henley in some circumstance could have revealed me dishonest, wavering, non-loyal to total dedicated behavioral compulsion belief only to Glenn Frey, my treasured seeking street drug of choice.

I don't mean I didn't support, follow, and respect Henley as well for I did. His was more financial. Roughly estimates out, I would predict to about ninety-one seventy-four a year for forty. But Glenn got my heart. That's a whole different involuntary addiction focus.

BTW, county music was a withdrawal measure gladly left behind in my biosphere with the passing of Conway Twitty, then Tammy W at only age 55

17

(on April 6th) and suddenly a few years later Waylon was gone. What a left turn the traditional country music scene had taken by this time.

Vince Gill once commented on the happenings to and of modern Country music "it's not my cup of tea" but that he probably wasn't Merle's cup of tea either at the beginning of his time and his attempts to be a musician…(Can't image anyone not appreciating Gill's voice).

Still, Alan Jackson was right on the money when he penned and sang about that little bitty murder that had gone crazy, brought a new rift, and was dancing all around down in the streets of music row. (I call modern day 'new-fangled monotonous country' as I can't tell anyone apart).

So yes, Alan clearly in the reality of my real world, what a wonderful day yesterday was…I was done with the country scene. Done, I tell you.

Music, like so many factors of life evolves, moves, flows onward. I adore music, love and can listen to most any musical style. Yet, this new country just wasn't classic 'my cup of tea' country either Vince.

In contrast, my generation didn't listen to what our parent's parents enjoyed. Some of their music choices were probably ok but most of it we felt was simply corny.

Music is a landscape of escape; an evolutionary movement that will and like the winds, must at times shift. Oldies move out and newbie come along. Each generation ID's its own types, sounds, and styles. I'm sure that's just natural.

Then suddenly, Henley made a new solo album. Oh yeah, thank you very much Mr. Don Henley. But lo and behold, it was country music. What, country? What a time of change.

Well, honey of course it's Henley, so we all had to have a preordered copy of 'Cass County'. Again, financially funding support and anticipated eagerness.

Now, what could the man not sing? That voice, what an effortless delivery! Just perfection-astonishing seamless flow. Don Henley is truly a standout; a rare one in a million not one of the million.

Henley's vocal cords would be interesting to examine under scope. They have to be in a class unique-O, unlike anybody else's cords. Personally, I would listen to Don Henley belt a tune from a Finnish encyclopedia (I know it's supposed to be phonebook but that's been used enough).

And wasn't some of the Eagles music aligned toward a country flare. Not just the Bernie style flare either, Hen and Glenn wrote some great music that reflected to the Texas southern realm of country and those Detroit roots.

Yet, I must honestly confess I hold a reinstated gratitude thanks to Mr. Henley for reminding all of us that country music can still be outstanding and almost as treasured as my smack problem for any Eagles song or their band member.

So, I guess now here in my real world I've somewhat gone back to country and that was a long way for me to go (ok, ok but thanks A. Jackson). Thus, to wrap it up in a nutshell just because of Henley my addiction stays alive.

Gratification, yes...but, that doesn't make Don Henley my pusher, right?

3: *Faith of the Eagles*
May 16, 2017, Opinion Contributor

As a youngster, I believed in and followed the teachings of my faith healers Don Henley and Glenn Frey. Two sacred icon cohorts, guiders-in-chief. They provided us so much spirituality and prosperous gifts.

Just for example, they taught us to worship the messages from afar, yearn to travel to the promise land-that being Joshua Tree, let go of and get over our misgivings, hold tight to our demand (you know like they did with that six-point five-minute song about a sleepover place in Cally). The iron men. Way, to hold on and stay strong guys!

The messages they shared seemed to make our lives deeper, more fulfilled. Those vocals, melody, arrangements, that attention to detail absorption of all intricate parts blend in order as a whole. The more the power rocked, the more we tapped in. The more we tapped, the more we enjoyed and like it all. The show men.

Yesterday, it was confirmed that some of the remaining youth ministers-I mean former band members are regrouping and, on the road, again furnishing more messages, concerts, music, magic, and memories. So, how will this be with Don Henley as the primary leader-the traveling man and no Glenn up on that stage?

As a disciple, I hold deep conviction to and in Henley. Thankfully, Henley has and always was a committed essential leader. The band just basically had Glenn Frey, the sports coach, redefining his team. And, as they both acknowledged, Hen simply stepped aside to the back seat to beat his drum. The wing man.

Now, there will be a junior Frey in training present. He's already rocked the house down in the past with Glenn which made us realize he can be an astounding upcoming musician and good fit for Eagles. And you know would make daddy real proud. The side man. The heirloom.

People comment about Deacon's young age. Well, I don't like it. So what he's young; as is that adorable Greyson Chance, spirited Harry Styles, & the incredible youthful Adele. For goodness sakes, have some reverence. Henley and Frey were young once and beginning on their fellowship. What a worship service they shared.

We all were young-once upon a time...some of us-long, long ago. They, as we all do in youth learned the ropes, turn the pages of the good books, improved overall, and grew in belief and understanding with age.

Thus, to wrap, I was and remain a devout follower from afar. I knew they would lead us down the path of righteousness. I believed, and I still do. Hold on strong, preach on Henhen. The lead man.

4: *A Year*
January 18, 2017

A year down the road why does the pain grow
a year down the road where does the time go
a year down the road our hearts are still heavy
a year down the road were you actually ready
a year down the road our world is forever lost
a year down the road the eyes pay the cost
a year down the road some souls remain tossed
a year down the road can't you just come home
a year down the road were all your seeds sown
a year down the road has the river run dry
a year down the road can an Eagle soar high
a year down the road does your spirit still roam
a year down the road will our dreams sing new songs
a year down the road our frozen lives coast alone
a year down the road how can a year already be gone?

* Glenn commented once in an early solo career interview "How long am I going to be able to go out onstage and play rock 'n' roll and look young and vibrant?" Well, tragically now we know and thankfully fans remember he was able to continue to play his music, look young, and be vibrant till the last onstage touring show ended in Bossier City, Louisiana July 29th of 2015.

5: *After Glenn Frey's Circle of Life*
February 16, 2016, Special Opinion Feature

Last night at the Grammy's the Eagles remaining band members Joe Walsh, Don Henley, Bernie Leadon, Timothy B. Schmit along with *"Take It Easy"* co-songwriter Jackson Browne provided a final surreal tribute to their co-founder Glenn Frey. Sadly, the circle of life for Glenn has ended.

I still can't believe it. Our Glenn. My Glenn. My knight in shining musical harmony.

OMG, an Eagle has flown forever out of the nest...how does that make sense?

A permanent change is in our mist. That change's icy cold fingers grip our hearts. We are here but Glenn is not. Why is it so difficult to comprehend or even think about a member of the Eagles not being present in the flesh?

Well, for one thing, it's a horrible nightmare. A broken circle. *"This has been a journey for me. And it's not done yet"* (Glenn Frey). But sadly, it was.

For another, it's only been thirty days to the date of public announcement, not even 30 calendar days...we still have two more from today to reach the 18th.

How did they do it, perform on that stage? These guys are made of some strong stuff; no wonder Glenn shared, loved, encouraged, and supported each one of them so fully. Look what they did for him last night. Moved that circle of life in his honor on in such an outstanding mean.

Full circle? Unending round ring. But why does the round circle have to have an ending point? Couldn't it just continue being a circle?

Life always seems more like a line to me than circle. Maybe not a straight line per say but a line with a beginning point and a final ending point. Arrival, departure. Date of birth, date of passage.

We all must pass. That is the horrible reality. But the journey is all about the 'stuff' that happens in between those dates, those lines. The stuff that fills the circle.

Boy, what a hole Glenn's circle made yet what a hollow gap remains in our whole world circle. You made that whole circle whole Glenn Frey and you made *us* entirely whole.

It's said losing someone forever is when you actually truly find them. I don't know but it really makes you realize what you had from their gifts.

Glenn truly had some amazing essentials things he accomplished, some challenges, some pauses, some breaks, rewards, and many major events on his roadway circle of life.

Of course, everyone's journey pretty much has many lines, events, avenues, exits, detours, hiatus lapses, side roads, off shoots. If life were a circle wouldn't it just be a clover-leafed section with no exit?

Why does life demand there be an ending part? Jesus, I don't want there to be an ending for Glenn Frey! And ending? Complete circle?

Will the Eagles circle of life as a band continue, or will it end (yet again & permanently)? What will happen to the 'Circle of Fear'? *'No music, no life'* (Tower Records, company slogan). I know I can't grow old without the Eagles!

Seems like it couldn't continue without Glenn. 'It' being the band or the music? Satan calculated something will be planned in the future. Unsure what to expect, not expect, or what that could mean.

An article in May 1982 alerted us of the actual fact on the band's first major pause breakup. Satan/Eagles manager Irving Azoff was noted to say "They realized they don't need the Eagles anymore. That's why you're not going to see them go out and do a **farewell** anything."

Upon returning for a reunion tour(s) and after HFOT boy did they do more and more Farewell's. Shouldn't Glenn at least have **one** elaborate some type of giant public special "Farewell Celebration of his Life?"

He deserves the recognition and appreciation for what he accomplished for the music world and his fans. One last respectful hurray? Who am I to suggest or consider what should be done?

But who would sing those Glenn songs? Who could succeed him!?! Who would want to play the role of our cherished irreplaceable Glenn Frey?

Everyone keeps pondering their questions and opines about the band. But personally, I think it's just too early, to raw now, at this time, for them to consider. Who could even have the heart to think about any of that yet?

Unsure how I would feel if they tried to move on without Glenn. "...sooner or later that's a stone-cold fact, 4 men ride out and only 3 ride back" (*"Doolin' Daltons"*). They need their personal space and time to grieve. Time will tell but for now it just doesn't seem possible.

Yet, Don Henley has always been a visionary, guider, and problem-solver. All vision and that future should be left primarily to his competent hands. Either formatted way Henley will let us all know when the time is right.

If they do anything hopeful it won't be years from now. Took Lynyrd Skynyrd time. Long, long, time. Ten years...lord our cherished guys will be eighty in ten years...

Don't know how my heart could take it if they do and/or if they don't-could a don't possibly be even odder. Time moves on. Life moves on. It seems to have moved on so rapidly.

Selfishly, I am just not ready for it to move onward. It doesn't seem normal. Guess I'm being a little selfish, but I need the world to stop just a little longer for Glenn.

Here, Glenn was this powerful magnificent creature that during his final act of mortality became fragile and succumbed, as we all eventually could as well. But back then, Glenn was the guy that every girl found charming and every guy wanted to be.

However, now, his inner light may have gone dark for some on or after January 18th but his courageous force, his commanding diverse voice, his exceptional musical talents, his profound presence will never dim for me.

Not to be to self-absorbed but been feeling like I was suddenly dropped into an open field in the middle of a harsh wintry night, desolate, deserted, lost, forgotten. Trapped, empty, aimlessly roaming in this deep isolated dark maze. No rescue. Or, like I was sinking while locked into a frozen quicksand path of liquid blackness disoriented unable to move, find salvation, or escape.

How can people get up and face each day, make plans, be normal? *"Our lives are changin', this old world keeps turnin'...* (well now it's come the) *time to leave behind some things from yesterday"* (Glenn Frey).

Naturally, situations are bound to happen in life that we hold no control over or could do anything about their occurrence. The French would state "c'est la vie"; that was the past, such is life, oh well that's the way the ball bounces, the way the cookie crumbles, get over it, forget about it, that's life. *"...this is the past"* (Irving Azoff/ Press release statement notation on lack of the band being present at Grammy's for '*Hotel California*' award win). But I can't forget yet.

Getting back to the grind, our day to day routines mandate this is what we must do. I am kinda embarrassed that I have such heavy sadness in my heart. This pain, too will pass? I didn't personally know Glenn Frey so why I am so torn apart.

Why does the pain feel unending?

Emotional teenage idol fairytale? Teen fever that we never really move past? We think we left it behind in that teenage world but is it like a virus, an internal element quietly hiding-waiting to elevate, to attack at any unsuspecting moment?

Last night seemed like such a graceful appropriate ending. It was so sad. Was this our formal way to say goodbye and end Glenn's circle?

Those faces screamed silent gripping pain for their brother and partner in song. When I looked at each face on the television screen, visibly there was such true penetrating sorrow for a dear friend, their beloved family member.

Their tribute was nice, simple, needed. Still there was a void missing...I yearned for there to be a single spotlight empty mic stand on that stage for Glenn-a light circling his space-seemed appropriate, seemed needed.

How are loved ones supposed to find the correct method to venture onward post grief? How do you cope? Therapy, meditation, drugs, group meets, praying to the great beyond powers to bring them back? How, why, how?

I know that we all always must move on. That is as life demands. But time doesn't stand still.

Spinning. Time, life, societies, generations, civilizations advance. That is, of course, the natural process, the order of things.

That human order to life that eliminates and demands stinks. It reminds us we are mortal and present too briefly. Selfishly, it often seems to jumble the process lending to rapid departure or too short of a time cycle.

The internal scars of grief are forever. The void remains empty lifelong. Just the slightly most unexpected thing can cause mental recurrence and instantly return one to gloomy emotion.

Time heals. Oh, please-really. Now does it or do we just learn that we must cope? Glenn detailed in an interview *time will sure change a lot of things.* Absolutely, it does change things; time's effect echoes those changes. Constant moving motion our changing circles.

Life is about constant change. Everything in life is in constant moving changes. Without change we cannot grow. If we can't stay current, we become stagnant. We do not learn. We become stuck and frozen in place. We're not living our one effort, our one chance at life. We will not move forward. Our circle would evaporate.

None the less, Glenn's family will slowly, eventually adjust to the lack of his presence. His children will continue their chosen path, probably graduate, plan outstanding careers, marry, have kids of their own. His circle enlarges.

But no one touched by Glenn's incredible life will ever forget him and his contribution to our world, our circle, our journey.

I am confident, as Glenn specified, during his last flight that he took that last *"goodbye look at America"* and as he *"said goodbye to all"* his *"pain and sorrow"* just before he *"stood in the light"* of that *"bridge across forever"* he knew.

For, likewise his America knew that Glenn had done good. *"To come; to see; to conquer"* (Vendi, Vidi, Vici/Caesar). He came along, he saw things in a different light, he conquered. Yes, he made 'it', he mattered, and he made a difference.

All the same, Glenn's life's circle end is unending. The legacy, music, journey, the children the brothers play on forward moving.

Over time Henley, Ms. Cindy, Joe Walsh, we all will march forward. That is the decree and power of the circle of life. The circle of the Eagles nest, unending forward band of movement...even after Glenn Frey.

GLENN FREY MAY HIS LEGENDARY MUSIC SOAR ON AND HIS SPIRIT REST IN PEACE AND TRANQUILITY.

6: *Life Alternating Commitment (Or the Who Lift!)*
February 5, 2009, Op Contributor

Every generation certain champions seem to hold a commitment to 'their' cause. We all need and seek relief. Our escapes. Our downtime, our release, our time away, time outs from the day to day stressors of life stress.

Some enjoy a devotion to a sports team, others rally political support, some love Star wars, rock climbing, James Bond, classic cars, photography, hiking, art, model trains, archery, puzzles, Dressage, the ocean, collect antiques, run marathons, hunt, follow theater, travel, build boats in the garage and so forth.

My dad held an unwavering love for baseball, especially Atlanta Braves chop-chop (and I think Cardinals, but he may deny St Louis). Mother's focus was children and piano(s). Her parents were dedicated to Christian faith, The New Deal, Macon Georgia Fuse Plant and growing anything from soil. A typical Saturday Evening Post kinda family.

While me and like-mines were a flock of formative wayward teen rock and roll music freaks. Like a Steppenwolf brat pack, seeking the adventure, we were born to play wild. Oh yeah, rock on!

We need those outlets. We yearn for that leisure retreat element. The time for carefree laughter and great fun-filled satisfaction. Just a downtime. Simple, laid-back, and exciting. Our outlet, cause, escape, our commitment, our *common thread*; connection connectors.

I won't even attempt or begin to explain each established following. It actually kinda makes sense in my feeble head why, where, and what we each treasure yet **_who_** influenced us may make a difference. But we all carried the torch without question, held our position gallantly and soaked in the enjoyment- which seems to be the most important release value and the clear meaning for understanding the element.

My pledge was influenced first by a kind-hearted, laid-back kid whom I was fortunate to baby sit. Thank you, Kirk Lewis, I am forever indebted, grateful to you who intro-'d me to the real music world of rock. And to your 'Lake T' mama who let us turn up the house stereo, the swimming pool audio, or car radio volume to max.

Or *borrow* her freezer dimes and quarters to play any type music we wanted on the skating rink or lake jukebox, over and over and over. (Freezer dimes, cups of coins in the freezer to make change for the cash register! Freezer dimes ha, that's what we called them.) Also, to Kirk's brother Tim who taught me how to rig a jukebox to get our dime back! (Dimes you can tell I'm old; remembering when pinball and jukeboxes cost went up to quarters).

Who would have thought that just by being given the opportunity to care for some young kids (despite the jukebox thieves that we *kinda* were) that simple task would lead one on a lifelong quest-a compelling devotion to rock, to Eagles music, and to Glenn Frey.

In our impressionable young fun-filled days me and those kids and any neighborhood groupie that dropped by were totally submerged by music. Mega stereos indoors, radios or boomboxes by the swimming pole, juke box in the roller rink, across the pond damn those lake speakers roared out the jive.

Later on, even as exciting was the rustic wooden plank open expansive western-theme style building those kids' daddy built in town for any weekend picker 'n grinner who wanted to drop by, sit on the bandstand, play a song or two, or just kick back and listen. All were welcome. Now, this establishment *"The Barn"* wasn't a joint juke or honky-tonk dive, just a gentle carefree styling atmosphere **where** no one was seeking stardom, only needing solace of song.

And, who but Danny Brown, rest his soul could have influenced me more greatly than by allowing me to tag along for my first concert to see Bob Seger in Atlanta. Truants runaways, yes, but who needed school we had the music pulsating internally to teach us all we needed.

My precious sweet always smiling Danny, I can see us now strolling down those halls of JCA (Josey Christian Academy) arm-in-arm singing Orleans *"Still the One"*, Seger's *"Old Time Rock N Roll"*, or *"hey, hey we're the Monkeys…"* and yes Danny Brown rest his soul will always be my dearest duet partner in rock N roll singalong. At least that boy could carry a tune…I will love and cherish him, his authentic friendship, and relish our music days until my last on this earth.

Thank you as well, Deejay Jim Brown, another patient who one that calmly listen to me drawl on and on and on about bands.

Influential who's as well included daddy's where a serious stereo system hooked to wiring running all over the attic to speaker boxes throughout the rooms in my childhood home.

In addition, Ed Powell's Record Shop for newbie and dated sounds. My parents, who both held love and passion of good diverse music, mostly country, gospel, with a slight flare for mystical crooners and heartfelt rhythmic soul. Ronnie Estes for graciously passing along tons of vintage 45-rpm, seven-inch vinyl records.

Arthur McCoy, known as 'THE REAL McCOY' an outstanding talented, wealthy, ambitious Davisboro, Georgia musician, who untimely, after cutting his first record was tragically killed in a dreadful horrifying accident. Growing up, it wasn't that I didn't know others who were or made attempts to be a sixteenth avenue singer of music. Some were just fine with being a small-town front-porch picker, lounge lizard, barn burning decent, mediocre, excellent, tone-deaf, or poor unassuming southern singer.

Yet, Arthur was of a different breed. He would have been a bright star on center stage. If he had lived and continued his dream for making country music in Nashville and beyond my life and career field would have detoured into a whole other realm.

Further mentionable 'who', that I would never forget to include would be Kim Kight. Kim the who that owned the cool portable turntable to spin records; for being my favorite dance partner, who always let me lead despite my two left feet, lack of skill, rhythm, grace, style, or coordination. Thankfully, Kim was as well a patience understanding music loving freak who took all those dance lessons and was naturally blessed as a poised hipster with great moves!

Head Coach Bernard Snellgrove, in align with a radio station in Georgia, who and where, I was gave me a unique chance to be an entrusted but poor-quality high school sports reporter. BTW, not sure other generations get the controlling impact radio stations and disco jocks held on the mid to late seventy's teenagers. Those who blew tracks into our wind, our ears listening for the music, and encouraged influential adolescents to keep reaching for the brightest stars and dreams. Dee jay super protagonist such as Kamel Amin 'Casey' Kasem, Shadoe Steven, Wolfman Jack, Captain Midnight, the Rick Dees pre-SiriusXM, iHeart, or digital age awareness, cultivated our static electromagnetic transmitting factual Wikipedia system on music and musicians.

Yet, the **who** that held the most powerful, profound affect and alternated my music life would include the thrill of when Glenn Frey lifted his head and locked those magnetic Windex-blue peepers into my soul. Impaled.

The moon and stars aligned, bluebirds sang, all was right-the enchanting spell cast. That was the begin of my story with Glenn Lewis Frey.

That lift lifted my soul to a whole new dimension. Of all the lifts, from all the stools, on all the stages from all over the world his lift revealed luring baby-blues that seemed to be speaking "well, hey there, here's to you kiddo." It was only the beginning of a splendid life-long bond.

LIFTED:

The stars aligned way up in the sky
when I looked up at the gaze
and that bright twinkle in your eyes
oh lord, oh my he's sent
from heaven on high
that's the way it was
meant to be
when Glenn Frey crossed my sight
caught up in the crossfire
he sang to my soul
he was a rebel warrior
and his command stopped me cold
it never was the same
it never was more right
than when he lifted his head
and locked my heart up tight
there'll never be another
here on earth that truly shares
his stage ruled the flying world
his wings flapped for my soul
he took the breath from my lungs
that screamed out loud and bold.

Lordy, life changed immediately on an imaged mental dime-forever baby; 4-2-1 *"the wicked wind whispers"*, *"out for a good time"*, *"take it up"*; *"shake it, make it, take it easy!"*

Now as a rebel mid-70's teen, I knew remarkable music well. Seger, Skynyrd, Otis, Doobies, EltonJ, AC/DC, Percy, Marvin, Cher, ELO, ABBA, Nazareth, Fogelberg, Sam Cooke, Joe Cocker, CCR, 3DogN, Queen, Tina, Righteous B's, Rod, Genesis, MarshallT, Steppenwolf, Benatar, Def Leppard, Bad Co, Journey-I could go on for days and days. A generation that knew premiere top-quality music. Classics, that transformed the roots of exceptional American music.

As for earth shakers of exceptional music, already I adored Eagles sound from those stereo records and the radio waves. Yet, with just a simple head lift-I was a goner. Now this lift happened during an instant of a *'Saturday Night'*. Thankfully, Glenn did not lift and begin speaking foreign Italian or I would have been on the next greyhound bus to LA and everyone's life would have changed on another dime, a more flawed one at best.

Back in my youth, working at Lake Tonya (a man-made beach, roller rink, bandstand amusement park type entertainment showground palace for teens of our community) we would take those 'zero' candy bars open the wrapper and place the bar under the French-fry heat lamp for a few minutes to soften. I thought I had discovered the eighth wonder of the world.

But I realized I was so wrong when I witnessed Glenn raise that head. OMG, a number one breathtaking wonder of all wonders. By my phenomena rank listing, I know *'who'* is the A numeral Uno natural modern day remarkably spectacular manmade wonder creation of the USA.

So, while today, I can listen to any past or present Eagle sing a tune especially the original four of Henley, Randy, Bernie or Glenn together or solo that *'one'* lifting look will always be a reminder of mine and Glenn's special moment!

I am confident he knew and felt it too!

Yes, in my heart I am totally that naive...

What commanding voices each singer held. The E musicians were made to make, play, and sing music. "Some mornings I've wondered. At night, it always seems right" (Glenn Frey) while in similar fashion Henley alleged, they had found their calling; yes, they definitely initiated their appropriate niche in life and music.

Every individual unique and prolific in their own right. I think sometimes

Glenn, Randy, and Bernie's voices were under appreciated because Hen was such a dynamic powerhouse singer. But so were Randy, Glenn, and Bern. Just replay their solo or lead tunes they really rock and shine, apart or together. Here again, we could go on and on for days... (haven't even mentioned duets or songs with non-Eagles...).

Now, while I may have a favorite *who*, there are Eagles concepts where I am torn. I often hear others comment on their favorite photo, concert, album, song, etc. I am happy for them that they can narrow it down and select as I hold no fav song, album, etc. of Eagles, Frey, or Henley.

They all are valuable to me for such a variety of different reasons. I could explain but you don't have that much time left on the planet.

Thank goodness I have lived long enough to understand and enjoy the meaning of valuables. As we get older, we comprehend the things that should be treasured. The worth of family, true friends, pure enjoyments, sheer privileges and you learn life is about character, loyalty, value, morale's, and the good things placed on your table.

My egotistic life's planet time has been simple. There been a lotta grins, much gratification, lots of nonmaterial valuables. All I ask now is to see Charlie become a Supreme Court Justice; Hunter grow up, receive his first Nobel Prize in Medicine, then I can get in the car drive to John Smoltz's, shake his hand, travel west to passionately kiss Tom Selleck. (Yikes, I'm really just silly and trivial, not a wack-o crack-o!)

After all that, I'll be ready to go on to the pearly gates to meet St. Pete and walk on those streets of gold while I await the arrival of my man Glenn Frey, so we can spend our eternity in music heaven! *

Hopefully, I did something somewhere kind enough for heaven's gatekeeper to forgive my jukebox thievery and school skipping dates! And it would be nice if Glenn could sneak in some of those 'zero' bars… *(is it wrong for me to hope they have candy in heaven?)*.

Thus, for now, I continue to proudly be a rock and roll music freak; Eagles music lives on as my greatest escape. My trans-fixational outlet goal line, raw electric energy that awakens pastime souvenirs.

In the same token, whatever your escape cause, give it your all. Don't look back Henley demands. And we all follow the beat of Henley's wise instructions. Thus, while your goal could be short, decades long, life alternating or for life- that's your call and forth right commitment decision ***whyever, wherever, or whoever*** it may be.

* Who had a clue in 2009 what horror January 2016 would hold for Glenn, his family, friends and his fans…?

SIDE NOTE: The Eagles band members often collaborated with Bob Seger and vice versa. On Seger's second album "Against the Wind" Glenn & Henley actually sang background vocals on this song of the same name. So, in tribute honor to that alliance, 'if only what we know today what wasn't obvious yester'.

7: *OMG, Glenn Dances on Stage!*
Farewell 1 Tour Live Concert
From Melbourne, Australia
~ *"To have joy one must share it."* Lord [George Gordon] Byron

Did you know Glenn Frey held outstanding rhythm and dance steps?

Yes, I know what can this dazzling human being not do? And, yes, we have seen some video's and moves where he swings and swags a little. But please tell me what the man cannot do exceptionally well.

The exciting film of Glenn Frey dancing to Henley and the Eagles band's during the song "*All She Wants to Do Is Dance*" from The Farewell 1 Tour in Melbourne, Australia (DVD, Warner Vision Label produced by our own GFrey) which was released 2005 is one invaluable breathtaking treasure. '*One, two, three, four*' Glenn wasn't the only one moving to the tempo. No cast of 'loiterers' could be seen anywhere under the roof, on stage or off, during those magical precious minutes.

This live tour, filmed at Melbourne's Rod Laver Arena in November 2004, is one of the more delightful events for the E band. Gosh, they all had a great time on stage during that performance; their singing sensational, their zest spine-tingling, their laughter electrifying.

Now, we know Glenn married a dancer, but did she teach him how to move? Of course, we see him on stage twirling about monkeying for Joe as well, but this Detroit born kid has some killer dance moves child. Gosh, it was heavenly!

On a side treat about this song, Danny "Kootch" Kortchmar wrote the song "*All She Wants to Do Is Dance*" which was sung by Don Henley our Eagles band main drummer and co-or primary vocal leader. *ASWTDID* was from Henley's solo album "*Building the Perfect Beast*" and the song was a triumphant success for Mr. Henley.

During the 1980's Eagles separation solo time Kortchmar wrote, co-produced, and played on many of Don Henley's songs with the albums "*Building the Perfect Beast*" and "*The End of the Innocence*". In fact, Danny K was co-writer on songs such as "*Dirty Laundry*", "*Sunset Grill*", "*Shangri-La*", "*Little Tin God*", "*Not enough love in the world*", "*Man with a mission*", "*You can't make love*" and tons more songs with Don Henley. (Mr. HenHen if I got any of this wrong please don't sue me-I am reading this info from your CD's son, and beyond thrilled to have each one and want you to make many, many more songs, recordings, and concerts).

BTW, just another interesting tidbit of info, I know fans would want me to share; Mr. Danny must be a fine young man even though he is a about decade and half older we have the same birthdate (hey so does Merle Haggard, ha).

So, at least for one thing, that tremendous dancing dude Glenn, talented heavenly Henley hound and Danny's marvelous writing skills eliminated or at least put that 'Loitering' gang of Eagles critics to shame and rest...Loitering impossible.

Finally, as our charming Glenn always does, he put those loitering commenters in their place, with just a few rhythmic pelvis moves and probably some fine whole-Detroit Frey words!

8: *The Music Had Stopped*

They broke apart we were told officially in May 1982. Our band had fragmented and split. Stopped. What? You knew if you were an Eagles fan there was conflict, tense times, and confusion-but to break up? Oh no, say it's ain't so Uncle Joe, say it ain't so.

Before then, out of the blue, right in the middle of any day or night, they made us feel things that we never knew. Only their music could read and find in our hearts an exposed script. Those E guys could, "no doubt about it.... they guided us" (GF).

As fans hung in there on their side day by day, night by night we felt it in our hearts as if our hearts were also on the line.

Currently my dear Buttercup Frey, is filling us up with new solo tunes. Ok, well the teenage heart throb appearance thing did change into admiration for their music, by about age twenty-five. That silly teen girl yearning to see the gorgeous one rock our world had turned into a respectful one for the love of that music. The heart and soul of their sound rocking our ground, our radio, our records, our arenas.

Yet, now Henley has released "*I Can't Stand Still*'and "*The Boys of Summer*" while Glenn has worked to give us *"No Fun Aloud"* & *"The Allnighter"* as well *"Soul Searchin'"*. Solo projects for each.

Does this mean our Eagles band mothership has landed, crashed, or just being maintained for repair?

Will it last, can they recover, overcome the past? Will it rebegin or will it end?

So, for today, I am thinking, thank goodness for their solo tunes. They are really great singers and songwriters together and apart. I am thrilled with their current singles or new musical endeavors, but you all know we miss our band's togetherness.

Yet, for now "those boys of summer" are men with their own vision and mission and moving up the charts.

They are 'soul searchin' while rolling out some great solo music assured and confident in their own skin, so we'll see about tomorrow (or an old team of band mates) may find a common bond and return...or find other roads and cars to drive.

But all the same, that *"True Love"* Buttercup is thrilling me with all these great tunes; E's and his solo music: *"Soul Searchin'"*, *"River of Dreams"*, *"I Got Love"*, *"Living in Darkness"*, *"Most of Us Are Sad"*, *"Livin' Right"*. What great songs (and of course many, many, more).

Music draws like a magnet. It compels and calls for reaction. Emotion. It jars us into reality or memory much like a sudden blaring earsplitting siren, a loud unexpected deafening gale force wind, a piercing crash of metal on metal, the thunderous roar of an intense ocean tsunami wave. It commands attention. It causes us to pause, turn, move, react.

The music blows with the wind, it flows through the trees, it dances in our veins clear as a crystal stream it courses through our existence. Enchanting and exciting music tosses out it's magic as a magician would. Powerful, mystical, captivating anticipation. We are awed and yearn for more tricks, treats, spells, and more hits.

Yet, what do we know, only time will tell but for now E fans are living in the suspense. They are at least a few interviews now and it's sound kinda impossible…but they are "the one(s) we love" so we just roll onward with the music they are giving us today.

STOPPED

Running in place. How do you stop,
How do you smell the roses, how do you not?
Why can life be so hard, why do we love sun?
What happens tomorrow, if we're suddenly done.

 # 9: *Could I dare compare Glenn to one of our Presidents?*
October 25, 2016, Op-Ed

Was it Glenn Frey or Teddy Roosevelt whose ideology was to speak his mind candidly, softly, and carry that big instrument…a stick for one, a guitar possibly for the other.

"It is not the critic who counts; not the man who points out how the strong man
stumbles, or…doer of deeds could have done them better. The credit belongs to the
man…in the arena, whose face is marred by dust and sweat and blood; who
strives valiantly…knows in the end the triumph of high achievement,
and who at worst, if he fails, at least fails while daring greatly."
~ (Theodore "Teddy' Roosevelt April 23, 1910/Sorbonne, Paris)

Anytime I read this Paris quote from our president, it reminds me so much of my own partial view on Glenn's personality. Or of what I speculate Glenn's philosophy for bravery in life would stand toward.

History reminds us that both Glenn and Teddy were as warriors leading the charge. Both were men of the new deal of their era and committed to the cause and value. Smitten by the wonder of travel, confident expressionist, second term and second chance risk takers.

Taking center stage one in charge of a nation and one in charge of changing the focus of LA country rock music sound. Recording of Theodore Roosevelts voice and speeches were one of the earliest presidents to be taped and preserved for posterity.

Thank goodness so much of Glenn's recordings we hold right in our own home today or can easily be found when we need to hear that voice or sing along....

Like Roosevelt, Glenn passed in January, both were competitive in sports, avid readers of books, visionary's, influential leaders, triumphant of many high achievements, each hit in the face during sporting accidents, had their own private memorial service, was set free in their sixth decade of life.

It was detailed Roosevelt was taken while he was asleep because he was a true fighter. Sadly, but bravely I think this would apply to our Glenn the fighter in the arena, the strong rebel, and that last both of these great men received honor medals from presidents posthumously.

Glenn and Teddy, Rough Riders of physical bravery, bold hero's, protectors, badland pioneer men, explorers of and travelers to the west, both outstanding men who changed their period of time on our planet and both hold stone or bronze statues on Mountains in SD or Streets in AZ.

Sleep in peace brave warriors, your spirits soar onward.

10: *Vanished Changes*

The desert flower cactus
sparkles in the sunlight
as rivers flow to streams
cool winds on the banks
wind blows out indeed
landscape harsh concrete beams
shadows grow to darkness
till blackness sews its seam
time stands still for many
since your left out of our dream
life moves on without you
but it's not the same for me.

11: *SHADES OF GREY*

The instant you departed
my heart was ripped in two
one side laughed of happy days
the other cried for you.
Taking it easy
was great to do
yet missing you brings heartache
that never fades away.
Memories stay awake of flights
we all took with you
but tears will often fall
remembering things of blue.
The moment that you left us
our world turns grey and black
one time was songs and tracks
now it's sad to mourn for you.
The day you departed
our world was ripped apart
as more grey cloudy days appear
tears rained down for you.

12: *Potentially*

Yesterday is now so far far away
from the sunrise that rose today
what will that light
shine down on our world
what will it bring fortune or peril
what lies in store no one will know
none of us here on the floor below
is guaranteed an hour's more show
so live life well
while you have your chance
the day will come when that chance
completes its last stance.

13: *Pondering resilience*

Go quietly into the night
screaming and kicking
falls out of sight.

Where do you go
and what's the demand
when life falls apart do you still stand?

14: *Cycles*

Out of the darkness
into the light
what shines
on your day
what makes it bright
where do you go
and what do you hear
how do you love
and who do you fear
what lies ahead
what's down the road
what leaves you cold
what makes you bold
is there a heaven
will it lift our soul
out of the dark
into the light
bring us comfort
on our last flight?

 # 15: *Vexing Forecast*

Shattering moments cause us to pause
cause us to stop, causes the center
of your world to stall.

Crawling out crawling from under
the weight of the earth
a sudden shocking thunder.

In your hand some destiny is planned
but other times the ruler commands
a crash down flashes that tosses you wonder.

Wonders of worry, wonders of sad
wonders of fate, wonders of mad,
wonders of joy, wonders of laugh.

But when it comes to shattering wonders
how do you cope, how do you accept
the chance blast by another dreadful conundrum.

 # 16: *SHATTERED*

Broken into pieces
shattered every part
fragmented fragments
ripped and torn apart.

Broken into pieces
lost and all alone
rigged jagged edges
without a way back home.

Broken into pieces
unable to repair
shards non-resealable
does anybody care?

 # 17: *Treasure*

A guitar pic
tossed from the stage
falls to the ground
for me
he was very different
from others
that we see
I hold that pic
close and dear
it reminds of a time
when songs rang forth
from our own
Glenn Frey's
cool satisfying mind
as now his soul's
flown free
to fly
high in the sky
where Eagles soar
in escape
of our questions why
just beyond our
great rushing
wind swept seas
beyond the clouds
up high.

 # 18: *Changes Never Stay*

Freezing a moment in time
capturing a feeling that all is fine.
Hope and determination, will it stay
will it be here if we face another day.
Could it all be gone
before the setting sun.
How could a life be suddenly undone
when all we yearn for is another day of fun.

 # 19: *Reflection*

What would you do
How would you know
Until you face your time
Are you prepared to just let go
To fly away or to stay
And try to fight another way
Are you anger, are you scared
Are you sunny, are you bare
Are you happy, are you free
Are you ready to let it be.

20: *Two Years*
January 12, 2018

January is our month for the beginning.
The future.
Empty slate to be filled with excitement, optimism, creations, new gifts.
The time for change.
The new, the start, the birth.
The chance for a fresh clean, stark blank page.
But then, came the wintry January of 2016.
The unforeseen new change exploded.

New news. Chilling blistery announcement of Glenn Frey's passage. Monday the 18th of that particular January.

In the blink of an eye, fate cast it darkest shadow.

As Glenn fan's, we were violently jolted; shocked, rattled to our core. Nothing seemed right. Instability ensued.

First month, first setback. Tragedy creating tragic reaction.

Some may have struggled somewhat or even on occasion experienced post-traumatic stress tears for this new, the bleak thing no one wanted presented. Presented about 'our Glenn'.

For of course, our Glenn was a rare global phenomenon. A powerhouse of royalty more than mere visceral cells. He was a genuine gift.

In general, gift is described as a thing willingly given to someone. A thing presented. In what seemed a very brief time, that wonderful gift, which was actually decades for many, was suddenly gone. Glenn Frey our gift, our presented present for that time.

At that point, I wondered, will anything in our world ever actually feel upright again?

After all, sharing his creation with others, Glenn made our small encompassing life balanced; more meaningful, fuller, tolerable.

And he held that relatable factor, a gift that connected us to him. Moved us. Our exciting, delicious fairy-tale. As fans we saw Glenn as cool, fearless, courageous. Our hip, energetic steel desperado with that striking star quality, an irresistible natural charmer who bedazzled.

Whereas now, another new cold January has arrived without our cool one. Anniversary returns, a season of change, which often includes some mark on our blank slate and possibly some type of emotion, both which may never truly leave us entirely.

This thing presented, that in reality we know cannot be exchanged, reminds. Yet, we understand that the 'almost famous' platitude truly applies here, as one can't change the action, but you can change your reaction. Even if it takes a little time.

For as time has passed during these two years, fans have probably worked that new news issue out of their system. Abrupt, harsh unwanted news. Bitter, raw loss.

In essence, with the emotion of loss, I have come to understand that loss is about the reaction to the old as well as to the new. The old gifts and some new gifts. *Some may weep that they "lost you, (others will gratefully) thank the stars above"* (GFrey).

Certainly, in loss you are forced to let go of what you must; purge to begin another start with the new. Dealt, healed, let go, moved out of the reaction's misery into to the new promised land.

It doesn't mean you must completely erase that mark on your blank page, it can be there in some form, you just learn what your need includes for the present. The present and the unfamiliar climate changes.

Naturally, the future moves forward. For, without moving we would miss out on so much of life. And, hopefully most have so much more living to do on this side of the promise.

So, on the 18th of January I will celebrate the amazing gifts Glenn's life unselfishly shared with others. For instance, the memories of his smile, that gorgeous hair, the music, those 14 scrapbooks (yes, I am one of those and the number is too high to list of tees shirts) the inspiration he motivated and over time, most important and very valuable to me, the way Glenn looked at his kids.

Just a brief beginning, but my gratitude list of Glenn gifts will be different from any other and that's what makes each so exclusive. Each adventure, each opportunity, each lesson, every gift special.

Moreover, I feel in my heart Glenn would want everyone to just eat life enthusiastically with a spoon and enjoy every drop. That was what he seemed to do.

And each of us do what we have to do. But you make the decision. Your choice. Your time. Your reaction. Your action.

You can boldly add some bright blended color to the blank page or simply leave your page plain. Just make the most out of the fresh new start. It's your one chance.

New time, new year, new ideas, new hope, new adventure, new opportunity, new page, new gifts.

"There is a higher power that guides each step of our journey. It will direct, lead, and push us through any element, be it storm, wind, sunshine, rain, snow-capped mountains, bleak valleys, grey clouds or blue skies. It's a force that can serve as a step toward a healing path and gently cleanse the soul."
~ (Anita G Shepherd)

SECTION THREE: A CELEBRATION OF LIFE

"But such is human life. Here today and gone tomorrow. A dream -- a shadow -- a
ripple on the water -- a thing...to sport with for a season...It is rough."
~ (Mark Twain), San Francisco letter to Virginia City Territorial Enterprise, (1866)

1: Remembrance: The Gift of Glenn Frey

November 6, 2016
Birthdate Year One

In my mind you never abandon the flight
you soar on, for you will never land.
You were incredibly brave, strong, fearless, and giving.
The one sliver of hope in a simple time gone mad.
Life can be fragile; life can be bad.
We will miss you sadly, but we are still glad
for the good things you gave us
impressive music you had.

The fun times shared,
the way you and Eagles cared,
'bout getting it right-perfections the word
every note was tight down to the chord.
For them Eagles flew proudly
as roarin' crowds
eagerly anticipated the front stage door
from down on the massive arena's broad floor.

That one larger than life was way more pretty
a sassy, talented confidence thrill of Detroit city.

A powerhouse masterclass motorcar followed the north star southwest
all the way to the Troubadour bar.
Many LA artists arrive or come and go,
yet we are so grateful, no we are so blessed
that you developed, arose, kissed, and sowed
in our twisted eras music city row.

Timmy, Joe, Don and Bernie fond brothers with charm
sang, play together near or behind.
Of course, we adore them for they were the kind
who knew as well how precisely to shine.
And it truly was heaven like ringing a bell
when you all joined voices perfectly pitched
singing joyously together
a cappella choices or solo tunes choruses.

Now life isn't meant to be breezy, but Eagles guys knew how to give
fans a brief time that was a feeling
to take it peaceful, to the limit, and stay easy.
Bathtubs were hazy filled with ice and beer
while all the cute girls laughed, swooned, and cheered.
Learning to power play some would say, dedicated bad boys wickedly tight
in stitched blue-jean britches one tough gang of musicians
really cool California transplanted Wholehearted Sons of ...
(Detroit half-word insert here)

Watching Glenn stand-out could drive you insane,
our senses churned heaven, skirting on fire,
tingling high alert burn to powerfully
rock us through countless festive hours.
While earnestly awaiting Seven Bridges of fame,
a spark occurs, match to a flame-igniting a blaze
oh, now what a pity, what a sad shame,
yet what a broad delivery what fantastic aim!

Your colors were bright
every night on the stage
mic at the ready, guitar in hand
pick tight between fingers
in glowing flood lights, you stand-
poised and steady.
It always felt right, 'cause you were the lead
ready, set, go we would all plead.

At any large cost, attempt, endeavor
never down for the count
a fine dedicated rock music tramp,
that teen king could make
any creative note solidly sparks, fly, vamp or bounce.
Yet heartache of long night, at a wrong beach
a low simmer burn erupts intense pounce
steering a solo stint as zooming dream careers churned.

True to your calling
fought the good fight
till hell froze over
saw it all in new sight.
But the famous return was a take it easy beat
that lead the band
back to their streak
and drove flocking fans up out of their seats.

Although to a Frey fan
your essence was more than cool class
one song moves us forward, one song yanks us back
into the rules of reality…a fast paradigm mask instantly turned upside down.
Despite sad frowns minor tranquility surpass
knowing peace for you at least has come to past.
Still in our youthful bittersweet fantasy you soar
singing brass, thunderous, and bold rocking stadiums galore.

But that final curtain call made our spirit sore
and left us stone-cold
standing alone in bad weather
yearning for one true last music measure,
seeking another sensational song
was that wrong that we melted faithfully like glue
to songs like 'Desperado' penned with golden throat guy
oh yeah 'secret weapon' Henley who?

Starring out from the spotlight hope you had a clue
the way we were moved how deeply we feel
how much we cared and how much we are scared.
That you suffered to strong,
held that stage too prolonged-
while we selfishly wanted
just one more long-lasting encore
and another thrilling Eagles Frey song.

Chilled as a Budweiser, sing middle C,
Glenn Frey seemed to be
everything we needed to see.
Now moments can be hard,
we want you to stay,
time brings us changes-shockingly cold
that seem to occur just beyond self-control
and life doesn't always kick a winning field goal.

My soul needs to scream loudly
"Glenn, please don't go"
except surely, I'm barred cause that's just too bold.
For we want you here man till we're all very grey,
till we'll all very old, if we only had our say.
Yet for today, we're still shaking and cold,
deeply scarred searching bright stars
and too often blindly losing our way.

But those cherished memories we hold are honors to unfold,
can continually be unwrapped, rewound, replayed till untold.
For those are priceless moments, incredible sentimental pleasure,
unsold values of wealth more precious than
vast tons of shiny gold treasure.
Then, through those treasures I recalled,
you didn't abandon, you simply gave us much, shared much
and through your music you actually captivated, inspired, impacted, rescued.

*We'll always carry a piece of Glenn Lewis Frey in our hearts. We move onward touched by his amazing contribution to the world. He enriched our souls with his exceptional music, determination, steel focus, his joy of life. When I first moved to the Pacific Northwest (Wonderland), I frequently heard hikers use the term' trail magic'. In other words, an unforeseen blessing, generosity, or kindness that occurred during their trek. It could be something as minor as a unique river rock, a nutrition bar from a passing stranger; stopping, lingering in the moment, perked on the ledge of an overlook soaking in the breathtaking majestic view, listening to sounds of silence, or a glorious Eagle suddenly flying overhead. 'Trail magic' memories. That is what Glenn was, an unexpected magical trail blessing on our musical wonderland journey. He made us feel better. But, like an Ol' 55 his time went too quickly. Without warning 'lickety-splickly' he had to be on his way. It's bittersweet to reflect on 2015; if we 'only' had a looking glass, psychic vision, or now a time machine...Eventually as they each leave, 'say goodbye' and as more and more suns come up, their star will begin to fade...While we wish they would stay at the parade much longer, it eventually can't be...But, once before 'our world was shaken', 'not knowing where we were going' we held on with and to our blessed desperados. We rode with lady luck, the queen of diamonds, and opened the gate as they drove us home... 'just another day in paradise'... ("Ol' 55"/Tom Waits, "Desperado").

SECTION FOUR: DON HENRY

"The difference between the right word and the almost right word is the difference between lightning and a lightning bug."
~ (Mark Twain), (1893)

 # 1: *Don Henley in Concert*

He walks onto any stage
and holds us in the palm of his hand,
we cling for every word of speech
and always yearn for more
his presence is oh so grand
his structure of poised plans,
southern goodness he stands
one so humbly ambient,
built of style and soothing grace,
holding court, having command,
his footwear just a dedicated tribute
to all hard-core working-class man,
we try to calmly wait
for his upcoming song
to hear his tempo beat
Seven Bridges till Desperado's complete
by which point we are all
simply up on our feet!

2: *Saying Thank You to Don Henley*
January 26, 2017, Solo Concert Review

Seeing Don Henley on the road in concert recently was a sharp reminder that we reached the mark of a year on the 18th of the tragic perplexing loss of Glenn Frey. Thinking of the sorrow that all had to face in this process especially Glenn's family and Don Henley, the past year has had to be difficult, stressful, trying days.

Thus, I feel a dire need to say thank you to Don Henley while we still hold the ability. Yet, I don't know how you say thank you to someone of Henley's talent, expertise, determination, and skill. It would be exceedingly difficult, intimidating, and humbling to try to compile. For all the years and accomplishments, he gave in addition for the perseverance and hanging in there with and for us over the years especially in the year of 2016, we are blessed.

In like manner, I would want to say thank you Mr. Henley not just for being an Eagle but as well for being an exceptional gifted solo talent, a devoted humanitarian and a strong, patient, brilliant human being. Most of all for the impact you made on '*our*' lives.

I have wondered of late what was it about the E's that was so mesmerizing? Now we had many, many sensational artists and we rode the wind and turn the page with them as well. What was it about Eagles that stopped us all in our track?

Was it the connection to the music? The words in the songs? The messages we thought E's were sending us, Don Henley's incredible enriching voice, their on-stage aura or OMG that Glenn was so doggone pretty! Don't know, don't care, and it doesn't matter now.

But what does matter is that in retrospect-I hope I am so, so wrong--I'm not sure Glenn knew how vital he was and how much people cared about him. So, it's critical Don Henley knows how important he is, how blessed we are, how grateful we are, and what he actually means to his fans.

Just a Branch of the Family Tree...
It was like Eagles were part of our universal family.
The music touched us on some personal level.
It aligned with our lives, shook-up our world, reached into our soul.
The guys seemed to understand & share our situations,
our thoughts, needs, and molded all that with
their experiences (?!?!) through musical expression.

It took me decades to realize how much I sincerely appreciated DH. In all those messages we receive---contradictions, deep meanings, reading between lines---sometimes I may have missed the point. "Silence is golden"- "Learn to be still"-Don't take photos- "Don't look back"! Wait what, don't look back?

Lord, Henley, if silence is golden, how do we hear the music? Learn to be still (then, bless his heart in seconds, he tells us to keep on runnin'). And this from the man that, thank goodness, isn't still but in relentless perpetual motion. For "only still can be still."

Actually, most of us know Don Henley is a genius and he is always right, but my thinking was he is just plain wrong about this one. Okay, so he's finally gone off the deep end (he could have stumbled across an ole stash of Uncle Joe's goodies). No son, always look back-no regret...

Sadly, it took a personal tragedy to wake my heart up. Now I wear that slogan (Don't Look Back) Tee shirt with more appropriate appreciation and understanding.

As for Glenn's tragedy, my heart bled for Henley and Glenn's family. I am so sorry for your lost son. I was devastated on January 18th, so I don't know how you all could stand it. I did not know that I revered Glenn Frey so much.

During this time, I tried to remember all the good things Glenn gave us, the fearless way he seemed to live his life, and oh my God, the way he looked at his kids! Those reminders gave me comfort. Glenn's life had vast meaning, carried purpose, and what a massive, imprinted legacy he left on this world.

And what an amazing mark Don Henley has made and continues to strive to make. If it were his music alone, that in and of itself would be outstanding. But the commitment, the dedication he holds in striving to make the world a better place, a far better than the one found, is highly commendable.

Glenn's shock was a vivid reminder to all the fans of how appreciative we are for GFrey and DHenley. Now, no disrespect to the others, we are nuts about them too; there was just something magical about that Henley/Frey marriage and everybody knows it. Despite the differences, the struggles, the challenges, the fame, the ego's they worked through and overcame. That's a powerful message to their fans!

Looking back over the long run, the Eagles had many revisions. That's life. I think the name Phoenix should have been considered! Still, I learned long ago Don Henley is way smarter than this one diehard moron fan, that he stresses (so we don't have to), considers all elements and everyone involved, and when he is done it is absolute sheer perfection.

Thus, to wrap-up, we are eternally grateful to Don Henley for every day, every song, every beat, every effort, every message, and every single minute. For the escape, the way and reason to unwind, and simply just for being you. So again, thank you, Mr. Henley. Stay strong!

3: *An Eagles Fan Runs Flying Down the Road*
July 24, 2017 Updated: August 2, 2017, Guest Blogger

Most of us are grey and just blend into the sidewalk. But, on rare occasion and a unique street you discover a shining bright star. A Conway T, Michael J, an Elvis, Shakespeare, Princess Di, a Tom Selleck, a Duke, Sally Ride, Adele,

Elton J, Babe Ruth. When we become lucky enough to get a walkway combo of Glenn Frey with Don Henley - Heaven is actually under our feet and we never take a noted minute for granted.

It, a lifetime of Eagles-mania, all started for most of us by a flock of winged warmed-blooded two-legged long-haired amphibians 'running down the road'. What road and why on earth did we follow is a forty-plus years trip.

None-the-less, every single day every spellbinding song, every decade was a musical journey, taking us on unknown roads, a street in AZ to a winding curvy drive into paradise. Whether down a long dark desert highway in an Ol' 55 or heading into a fast lane, we tuned in to the taps, sang along, as we rode each curved miracle mile. And, when a young-blooded diehard checked in or jumped in we didn't want out.

I suppose I just take it for granted that every single human that has ever breathed breath knows that Henley and Frey are the musical co-founders of the biggest selling American band of the twentieth century.

But if you need to Goggle them be quick Henley is now 70 yrs young, and sadly our beloved Glenn is no longer here on this side of our highways. (Just please don't mention to Don Henley that I used the word Goggle! Just kidding, Henhen, just kidding, son).

Recently this committed total 'Glenn Girl' fan took yet another trip and flew into Dallas for Don Henley's 70th Birthday bash. Stagnant air doesn't get much heavier, bone stifling dry or sweat drenched humidity rise much thicker than when you are in Texas in late July and Henleyville is in town for a whirlwind mind-blowing concert, a birthday celebration and a private meet-n-greet.

Now, for full exposure I have had the incredible privilege of meeting Hen before and am truly thankful to have seen him in many diverse venues. He is one Southerner that never disappoints, gets right to the heart of the matter, always goes above and beyond any expectation and delivers us all to an endless serene highway, foreign, or known.

Yes, that is not a typo Henley is from Texas. I understand, I too being Southern born and bred always think who on God's green planet from east Texas sounds like this man!

But, back to focus, the bash began with vintage varied radio waves from rafters-what tunes, what messages, what a diffusing reminder of Henley's brilliance. Many attended the gala. Big time celebs Patty Smyth and Stevie Nicks arrived in grand fanfare to provide B-day praises and superb chart-topping hits to/with Henley. Of course, other Eagles, Timmy and Walsh whom we adore, as well were in attendance for this incredible event. Kinda odd to see Eagles perform with no Frey in tow. Bittersweet, but we didn't focus on abstinence and soaked up the enjoyment.

Henley sang beautifully-ravishingly perfect, and he drummed! Patty in a sparkling silver 'disco ball' jacket, (guess she visited Uncle Joe's wardrobe department) the band, backups, the musicians, Stevie beating the tambourine were in the same rare astounding form. It was a remarkable impressive party time in partytown ending with a Beatles ensemble treat and white balloons raining down from those rafters.

Is there anyone on this side of reality humbler, striking, or gifted than D Henley? That stirring voice, that insight, that mannerism, that talent, that presence unparalleled.

I fumbled highly intimidated to try with poor attempt to explain to anyone within earshot of what he and especially Glenn meant to me in my past juvenile smitten silly lifetime of years ago (whew, thank goodness those type years are over and I 'a' adult now!)

As for the following day, so much occurred that it would take weeks to cover. One thing he did mention was that he now has a voice coach to assist with getting his beat-up voice back in shape and prep for shows. Wait what, a coach to help Don Henley with that voice. Oh Lord say it ain't, so Joe-please don't change a note.

Yet, probably most important to me was simply seconds at his right hand. Henley always seems slightly nervous when I speak or get near him (ok probably just bored). Honestly, I did beg him to smile at which he replied, 'I am trying darling'. Words we live for and thankfully not "Security!" Bless his heart, I know he wanted to run back to any highway and face the big trucks on a twelve lane rather than be forced to stand there calmly, patiently, warmly smiling with a simple minded red head. Guess after all these decades he has learned to be still...of course I do declare he is as always, a true Southern gentleman.

How is he supposed to look into our heart and understand? Of course, if anyone could it would be Don Henley (if you are a stanch Hen fan, you get that!).

Now, Henley is moving forward yet again. Or will he stand still? Enumerated last year he was considering a soulful album of sorts, no remark on this potential. But that would be absolutely amazing. He holds the riveting treasure of that raspy liquid tenor voice created to belt out blues or peel Lucite paint from the walls. Listening to the man sing *"Hold On I'm Comin'"* or *"Midnight Hour"* blows your lugnuts right off the tire rims-it maybe the ending yelp that grips ya.

Not that every message the man writes, or sings isn't simply pure heaven. A voice coach-really? Please. He is an icon and truly a musical genius. There is a reason his greatest enemy named him Golden Throat.

He has quite a zest for life, music, the wide-open lanes, and byway like so few probably could still handle at seven decades. Which as he calmly explains and shrugs *"it's just a number"*. Hmmmm, 70, just a number?

Thankfully, he is still crafting astonishing songs, holding court, running down the road and fulfilling dreams-his and ours.

Henley updated Classics news on Seattle and Atlanta (he 'thinks') with

Doobie Brothers later in the year with possibly more dates/cities to follow. Well, more we all pray.

Currently, Henley is in middle of the Classics singing with his chosen Eagles team band, which began last weekend and included Glenn's son Deacon Frey and Vince Gill. Of course, it exceeded all expectations.

What an outstanding, start-your-engine revenging opening Deak contributed. Roar on 'Small Frey'. He pushed the metal to the floorboard- as they all did. What a show! It's thrilling to be witness to a new birth with Deacon-right there beginning a future full of promise and possibility. Gosh, what another amazing side road or new path on the ride's journey!

Personally, at first, I had mixed complicated emotions about his decision for the band's future. Not bitter, delighted, anger, ecstatic feelings, hooray just odd feelings. And who on earth would ever judge Don Henley or any choice he makes in life?

Well two years ago they were done, now they're back (briefly?) they're singing on stage today, they could tour or not. Well? Well...

Just sometimes with the Eagles you ride the emotional roller coaster. Sometimes it can be a smidgen tense.

Still we're here waiting; bated breath. Often, waiting while biting our fingernails to the quick. Anticipation rising, fear of another unexpected "great, I can't wait" moment. But we still hang on to the top rim of that stage floor clinging by the bloody stumps of our nails.

We hang on in there with them "tooth and nail". Our band. Our men. Our bond.

Anticipating the thrills and unknowns. Up, down, curves, highs, rapid drops, twists, slows, stops.

At Classics event, Henley did address as before this ride could wind down to the end of the line for the band. Scary thought. I always fear Henley is not going to get off the road and in the same instance I am petrified he will get off the road!

What if he does? Would he still solo? Could Henley take an exit route, a detour and never come back? Well, I'm back to the roller coaster. What would we all do this time if the band took another 14-year hiatus?

Henley has said in the past at times this is our last hooray. We all know he will tell you he has changed his mind before. Then, in Dallas he states (thankfully) "I'm not done rocking." Lord, son you are killing me! But I just keep paying for the token and get back on the ride with all the steadfast loyalist.

This exciting ride has been up functioning for a long, long time. Could it start wearing down? Repairs and modifications have been constant, but will the coaster be plowed over for a newer structure? Could it check out or end-up at or as the Last Resort?

Now I am thrilled that he is considering doing what he loves, taking others along for a ride even if it may be a short trip. Or taking a much-needed well-deserved break if that's his choice.

As for putting Glenn's son under his wing in whatever fashion, for this one thing alone I feel Glenn would be smiling and in complete agreement. Henley mentioned in Dallas how strange it was to go on without Glenn; and that from his drum playing panoramic-perched view of Deacon on stage (& the hair) it was "heartwarming and freaky at same time." Deak will be a greater asset in any form to our cultural music world.

And, Deacon Blues has sung and played with Glenn from the time he could stand up right and hold a guitar. The teacher and the student. If anyone is ready and able to follow closely in Glenn's footprint, Deacon has been preparing and prepared well by Glenn's lead and guiding hand.

However long or brief Deacon makes a solid professional choice teaming up with Henley just like his dad did so long ago. After all look where it took daddy.

Henley will metaphorically take Deak's hand now, mentor, continue to assist his pal's son toward his destined path. The masters and the novice. The legends and their beginner.

The Frey torch passes.

Yet, Eagles doesn't seem to be Eagles without Glenn. Nobody will ever be Glenn Frey.

As for this staunched loyalist, I have learned to take what I can get while it's running down the road. Maybe that's settling and we all know this band don't settle.

Deacon's not Glenn, but that's understandable and no one should expect Glenn reincarnated. He's first class assuredly or Henley wouldn't allow him to be a new addition...or a part of whatever is ahead.

People came and people went separate ways with the E's. Bernie Leadon left; here's Joe Walsh. Now that was quite a reincarnation! That took a while for adjustment. To say the least, I was rather ticked with Glenn. What are you doing? Yet, that shift added a whole different cart to the amusement park adventure.

Walsh brought a strange trip to mid-70's style fear-attempted fun, rare shenanigans, debauchery sliding and possibly vomiting (not the Timothy/ Henley joke, the Joe conquered and survived raw paraphernalia). Selfishly, I adore Bernie and always will-yet, now I can't image the ride without Uncle Joe.

That speaks to what a visionary Glenn was. Then Randy walked, so into the mix came Timmy. Changes occurred, decisions recast, but the same music played on. However, that sound will never be echoed again live. Never, period. January 18th that music ended.

Prior, much has been framed on Frey hand-picking ever single member associated with this band. Henley, Walsh, Timmy, Satan, even Bill Szymczyk and Jack Tempchin. Ok, so maybe Henley was a packaged deal as far as the early Glenn outlook but what an incredible packaged gift!

So, as an outsider looking in, I believe in my heart that Glenn is content and highly pleased with all of Henley's hand-picked decisions. That's what matters most. Whatever they develop into or not and wherever the destination leads or not...revisions, that's life.

I have learned Glenn Frey and Don Henley are extremely wise men. In hindsight, Henley is conscious of every element, observant and always seems to make the best decision for the band, the fans, and for himself.

Thus, when you find something on life's path that is not illegal and you enjoy, you should jump on the band wagon and take off down the road, don't look back, learn to be still, enjoy the silence. Henhen articulates it's golden.

If you are an Eagles fan like me, as should be evident by this point, you know first there is no *the*, you probably understand how to enjoy the music and the silence, the road is nearer the end than the begin. And if you love this band, want to see these bright shining stars fly while singing as we drive down the music row of life, you should get there now. Sadly, that road may dead-end one day and it could be real, real soon.

No regret here in my bland corner on my dim destination blended into the pavement musical journey, except in the tearful devastated Glenn department and that's a whole other atlas for another mapped passage travel on the vast Eagles highway...and I may have more words to communicate on that voice coach decision...hmmmm interesting...well another token for our colorful amusement roadway.

4: *Don Henley Has a Voice Coach* (*I said there maybe more*)
August 10, 2017, Op-Ed

I said I **may** have more to say on this subject. Well, today for the third time I have to comment on Don Henley's Dallas Birthday events; now on to the subject of his voice coach. More specifically, after reading the incredible blog posts that Debbie Kruger complied on the events, the Birthday concert, the rooftop party, and the Q&A segment, I had to finish what I had started on the matter of voice.

Yes, this was a great article on her review of Sunday's Q&A (actually she had more than one also, ha). I read everyone's material possible afterward and Deb Kruger's were extraordinary and richly detailed.

And she was the young lady that day, out of the entire Q&A marathon session, who caused a catastrophic horror for me as she asked Henley about emotion during singing.

Or well actually, Henley reply was 'the horror'.

He, of course, calmly commented he now has a "Voice Coach" and they were telling him he was singing "all wrong". *Now, that dog won't hunt!* If you are not southern, that means those words just don't make one lick of common sense.

It was actual physical will plus almighty God above that held me in my chair and prevented me from screaming "OMG, what a VC? Singing wrong!?!?! I will kill them if they alter that heavenly blessed gift from on high." It's DH-'wrong'. Wrong, please. Wrong, how does he sing anything "wrong"?!?!?

Because of my complete frozen shock and before I could jump to my feet, commit sin, or have security drag me out of the building, Henley went on to mention they as well swore their involvement wouldn't change his tone/voice box. And, if it did, **he would kill 'em**-whew thank goodness I believe him. God, I pray for their sake they don't have to deal with a Southern Classy Redheaded

Henley fan. Bless 'em--you know killing 'em just wouldn't be good enough if they damaged our HenHen's voice.

A voice coach for Henley? Isn't that's about as useless as an ashtray on a motorcycle? "Whatever" (ever notice how often Henley says this or am I one compulsive attentive DH listener-yeah whatever?).

Like most E supporters, I could just listen to an Eagle's powerful captivating chit-chat all day. Particularly, Henley or Glenn. For obviously, Don Henley and Glenn Frey were the Holy Grail of all voices. (Yes, in my rose-colored world).

Off topic, I recall a big wig refer to Alan Jackson's songwriting skill as 'imperfect' (what!). He commented to Jackson something along the lines of you can't write like that, you don't use the same word in the next sentence and there has to be a certain flow to wording and writing. For example, June can't follow June, or you can't wear boots while water skiing.

Then, he watched what Alan did with his thought process, lyrics, his music, and it all in some tactic worked flawlessly. He laughed and said suddenly, he realized Alan knew what he wanted to do and that he needed to leave that boy alone and let him do his thing. (Amen sir).

That's what I would say to any advisor for endorsing Henley's need of a voice coach; but what do I know.

Refocusing, it was a wonderfully entertaining weekend. And DH, who was in rare chatty form, seemed to enjoy himself as much as everyone else.

Henley and Debbie are both fascinating storytellers. And she explained something I totally misheard on the soft-spoken word sad verses mad, oops, so that was good.

Overtime, it took me a few reads of various articles from Henley Runaway events to realize certain reliable individuals had to be provided transcribes and I am truly grateful as so much occurs you never remember everything (Yet, I think we as the audience are supposed to be dumb and/or silent on this action).

Anyway, someone in the crowd made a comment to Hen that he was the nice guy that didn't have much to say in public and that Henley appeared to have changed in the open public setting. I totally agree. To which DH stated he had mellowed, was more comfortable now in his skin, and had grown into himself.

Everyone under that roof was transfixed. HenHen of the past was usually a rarity on the interview circuit, is a very private exclusive person, and seemed to avoid public forums as much as possible.

DH is extremely, extremely, extremely intimidating, one very serious dude. I mean extremely. But, for any of Henley or Glenn's advent followers, when they smiled or laughed it would light up the room and our hearts and our universe.

We knew that we all were expercing a Henley rarity. Don Henley at his best. He was lively, enthusiastic, hilarious, charming, open, sharing, at times unpredictable and uncharacteristic in discussing many things that are often very off-limits for him.

Maybe, he did open one of those presents Deb mentioned and it was a good one. I don't know if he was just in an ongoing wonderful Birthday mood, still high from the night before concert, yearning for all to enjoy the day or if maybe he, in his aging wisdom, (Can he get wiser?) is releasing that silence is golden rein just a slight, slight smidgen.

Didn't matter to us, it was one unmatched special Birthday present memory for enthusiasts.

Moreover, it seems he has evolved more toward openness especially after Glenn Frey's situation. But maybe it was just one of those really blessed days.

All the same, we were humble and deeply honored to be a part of that historical moment in time. Grateful to and for Henley; grateful to Debbie.

Well, guess so far this really hasn't been about the voice coach. But I will be keeping my watchful overly sensitive Eagle eye on that matter.

Guess, it was more what Debbie inspired me to rethink. Deb, BTW, has a phenomenal rhythmic style and talent with her words. (Check out her blog, if you adore good writing about music/musicians, you will love it.) Unlike any of this jargon, she is a real writer!

Like Hen, she is a true voice artisan on the word works. And, Debbie, child, to compliment you I loved and applaud your singing *"Desperado"* on the bus! I almost cried with your words. I could clearly see how it meant nothing; yet everything.

And I agree with you entirely sister, Henley is wrong-yes of course I know Henley is **always** right, but he didn't need to re-record that song. It was perfect in voice (no coach needed, umpty-umpth) as I am sure your version was as well. So, thank you DK for sharing your outstanding passionate writing and sometimes singing skills-she always makes you feel like you are live in or reliving the moment(s).

As for growing up around and later living in Macon, Georgia I was greatly pleased with Debbie's positive passionate love of Otis Redding. And further, as she ascribed and longed for *"Waiting in the Weeds"* **yes, please Don Henley**. We _also_ long to hear live in concert *"The Last Resort", "Learn to be Still", "Wasted Time", "Words Can Break Your Heart", "Busy Being Fab", "How Long", "New York Minute", "Hole in the World", "Dirty Laundry"* and by the way Henley whatever happened to *"Saturday Night"*? (Ha)...as well about four hundred other songs but I know there has to be a limit somewhere to that setlist.

Just trying to help Hen with suggestions…

If I could truly make a proposal for a concert, I would have to recommend that Henley allow Deacon to do a legacy tribute melody to our dear Glenn. Like maybe snippets of, *"Soul Searchin'", "The One you Love", "The Heat is On",*

"The Good Life", *"River of Dreams"*, *"You Belong to the City"*, *"Here's to the Good Life"*, *"Part of Me/Part of You"*, *"Smugglers Blues"*, *"True Love"*, *"All Those Lies"*, *"Wild Mountain Thyme"*, *"Somebody Else"*, *"She Can't Let Go"*, and bring it home with *"Heartache Tonight"* (yes, I know that one is on the setlist).

AND some oldie background pictures of E's AND more Hen solo songs as well would be nice…just giving HenHen some advice, doesn't mean he has to listen and would he anyway…I just like the suggestion *possibly*.

Soundly, one comment Debbie elaborated well upon was Henley's response to a question on his bucket list. I have much to say about this response as well. His discussion and her descript of his magical childhood corn field and 'Dreamtime' was remarkable, his dynamic follow-up unforgettable.

However, all these years I have been lost in the weeds thinking *"End of the Innocence"* was about sex. I know I am not the only one. No, no, no-way, no I am not. Getting lost in that maze, lying on the ground, hair spilling round, ending that innocence.

Like a prolonged lingering layer of thick fog that refuses to lift (another '*lift*') that stunning layer of childhood innocence lingering. He commented how he loved as a kid the serenity of lying on his back in the dirt looking up through the corn stalks and tassels as the clouds roll pass.

Lying on the ground he found peaceful easy moments frozen in mental timeframe. Ending the innocence, like a layer of shiny lacquerer stripped away, leaving exposed the raw plank of reality. Great that he cleared that up.

He is the man that states he has a love for hidden meaning. In my view, I would have thought a southern Texas corn field could only serves as a reminder of scorching heat, dire itching, and hard work. (The pessimist girl verses that optimist golden throat dreamer).

Still, Lord, how off-base can you get?

Anyway, one bittersweet notation for me was Henley's mention of travel with his kids. The places he has been, but while places he was truly present, he said mostly he was unable to visit properly due to touring schedules, time, and need for privacy.

When on earth can you do this, son? We are not going to allow you to take a break, please. You had that break the whole Eighties. Hope you enjoyed. And your current bucket list is like 70 million miles long!

Sincerely, I do hope Henley gets to see this materialize. He and those kids deserve that together real travel vacation retreat.

Here is a man that gives deeply to society, music, and his admirers. He is on the open road so much. I have often wondered what type of real life this is, the success, the records, concerts, interviews, rehearsal, the work, work, work. I know everyone thinks this is a glamorous lifestyle, but boy it sounds rough.

He has anything money could buy (well, except that corn field, God bless him) but does he really have everything of a valuable life? Is he happy? He just seems sad sometimes. Just my thought, only privy to his professional side of life, so surely, I'm probably wrong. As delineated, he is one serious guy.

One thing Deb and I can agree wholehearted on is Henley has the musical thump pumping in his blood. He'll never stop making music. That's the sign of a truly solid dedicated musician.

Two things I did disagree with DK; one, for once Henley did seem, especially at times, to shockingly really let his guard down. And that was a different Don Henley than I have witnessed. He and everyone attending wholeheartily drank the enjoyment of each relaxed, exciting minutes inward.

I never thought I would hear Henley utter the words 'fuddy duddy', now that's laid-back. A true southern gentleman showing his roots. Fuddy duddy; I honestly heart Don Henley!

But as for relaxed, maybe others that know him well agree with her on

71

thoughts of his unwavering stiff composed reserve (my words).

The other, I floated him a psychic thought and he caught it in air mid-drumbeat. Or in other words I _mentally_ demanded about thirty years ago that Hen blend-belted voices with Steve Winwood as well cover 'Tears for Fears'.

Sorry Deb.

You're welcome America and beyond!

And he listened. (I know it was all me, don't you feel it too!)

From the first time I heard "TforF" in the mid 80's on the 'radio' wave lengths (& later 'Steve Chappell and the Bulletz' @ the HonkyT on Gordon Hwy in Augusta, GA*) sing "*EWTRW*" I knew that song was made for HenHen's incredible, powerful full-throated voice.

If I can just get Henley to hear my mental vibe about Dire Straits/"*Money for Nothing*", Mavis Stapleton/"*Take U There*", EltonJ/"*Sacrifice*", MGaye "*Sexual Healing*", Sam Cooke/"*Bring It On Home to Me*" and Cinderella/"*Don't know what you got...*", my own pretend daily happy list would be done...(ok, maybe a few Elvis tunes of his choice).

I was right way back then, that southern Texan gentleman needs to listen up!

Just pause and think about that Don Henley voice and these noted selections.

Actually, to be honest, that 'Henley has to sing record list' has 192 other songs but I will just leave this alone, *for now*. Wonder if I should take a moment to mention the blend duets Henley should consider with Adele, Steve Perry, Joan Jett, Brian Johnson, Anita Shepherd...

Aside, he seems to have done pretty doggone well with his own musical creation, thought process, and direction!

As for Henley performing the song "Everybody Wants to Rule" ever notice how **any** audience reacts to this song?

Personally, I feel people respond to the beat; the tones of the beginning

72

notes blending with the melody. Listen to the first drum pound, a chord or two, the guitar riff, music scale, the bar/the measure, a touch of a few piano keyboard notes, the saxophone, the melody prep *then* the lyrics commence to roll or whatever means the arrangement begins its flowing journey.

Sound effect? No, sound affect. It heightens the adrenaline rush; the anticipation and we respond because 'we know' what's coming.

That's all that needs to be stated on that musical tune.

I apologize if I offend Debbie with these personal thoughts and comments for, I do vastly respect and appreciate her written voice. I am sure by this point in her writing career she has tough skin. And albeit, what I know about music, musicians, writing, or Don Henley won't fill a thimble.

Surprisingly by chance, Deb ended one piece of her work on Henley's voice by commenting that Henley held a voice that melted people's inner core and that we all pray that voice will never go silent. Amen girlfriend!

Plainly, that girl doesn't need a voice coach. Like Henley her words, her declared voice, her vocal style is shear perfection. No need to tamper with shear perfection. Now, if I could get Henley to understand this last vibe hell might freeze over again.

5: *Watching Henley Accomplish*

In his shadow we all stand
highly intimidated
by the front back man
in his shadow down on the floor
we watch him function
and pitch a chord
singing song or beating drum
that's what he does that we all love
highly skilled amazing talent of show
performed for us front to back row
in his shadow and on his stage
are true believer
and those that brave
every element every worth
for his time for his plan
to give to all one last command
yet in his shadow we all stand
in his shadow but he's just a man.

6: *The Henley Rarity*

There are not Don Henley's born every day.
They are a rarity that when found need appreciation.
DH was born to change the world.
But do they feel they are born to change?
Is it from a built-in drive or does it develop overtime?
His talent, ability, skill, knowledge, voice.
Why would he share it and why ask why?
We should enjoy it before it leaves for goodbye.

7: *The Gifted Power of the Voice*

> Henley's rare voice is a deeply infused instrument.
> It carries energy, soul, and emotion to the surface.
> It's a stunning tool; furnishes authentic essence
> that can plug in to touch, provide
> raw powerful moving expression.
> Every time you hold the treasured opportunity
> to hear it, you are reminded you are being
> rewarded by a special shared unique gift.

8: *Woven Dreams*
July 20, 2014, Op-Ed

Don Henley is a dream weaver. A mystical soul in a state that can do anything to dreams. And, when your realistic dreams come true, they always include some sweet ones.

Some dreams may never happen, some dreams you lose. Some are warm, strange, exciting. Some dreams are restless, a few can make your pulse race or be frightening nightmares. However, some dreams you conquer and when you win it's divine.

Essentially, Gary Wright was the 'dream weaver' songwriter, Paramhansa Yogananda's poem set the idea, and John Lennon self-declared himself as the sixties dream weaver. But for many music fans, Eagles were our dream weaver.

As for the E band members, they may have started off as Linda Ronstadt's back-up team but as a group they took off in-flight for their dreams on a high chord. Later, Linda verbalized that Eagles band is "stunning (live) in concert". Above all, she is right and she should know.

Chiefly, by intertwining words, images, insights, melody, meanings, concepts of intuition the band furnished a magical music journey. The possibility, benchmarks, their goals, grabbing the brass ring, well they certainly achieved and "then some".

But that journey wasn't without bumps, ups, highs, lows, sleepless nights, major records, energy, trial, tribulation, thrill, motivation and some downs. As well in their case, well-documented downers, crashes, loves, some outstanding achievements, a pinch of bitterness, some awards, rewards, a chunk of money, wine, women, and song.

Major experience having your dream come true.

They were 'defined' by floor to ceiling music, woman, booze-a-moola, tours, spirits, tiffs, attention, and huge success. Those musical weavers began the seventies with a history-making journey, hip-style dreaming desperados, hard-hitting ambition, hedonism on a razor's edge, humor built from the cracks, hate boiling at times, hormones on overdrive, hot sizzling young hotties, hell on wheels, 'horrible reliefs', hell freezing over and huge hits in the making that still today are categorized as the soundtrack detailing our lives.

Both Henley and Glenn, were by all count, righteous self-disciplined perfectionist (Randy said Henley was a "*stickler*" but that he meant 'in a good way'). In my humble two cents worth of opinion, Glenn seemed to be the one with the largest vision, drive, and overarching power for the directed path. The others of course were absolute crucial elements, but Henley and Glenn seemed to me to be the reassuring central core glue. Yet, the heart of the music appeared to be Henley.

The challenge was their joy, the process defined this professional family, their attention to detail and focus was grounded in their music. Each one has an incredible body of work. And all of Glenn or Henley's songs, absolutely each one, whether in a band setting or solo holds water.

Moreover, many of Henley's songs have such obscure well-intended hidden meaning. That unknown obscurity drove us like a crime investigator with an intensity to solve; but in actuality we never will. Those aspiring songs helped us get through our pain and help us control what was going on in and around our lives.

Many say their favorite Henley moment came on E: HFO (*'Hell Freezing Over'*) taping April '94, when during *"Learn To Be Still"* Henley **paused** over the wording 'sheep without a Shepherd.' Upon viewing this performance, I knew that it had to be a well-planned setup, right?

We all know the world's greatest perfectionist would *never* pause or stumble. Oh, yeah it was exceptional, finally we realized, my gosh, Don Henley is human!

Of course, I jest, for surely it was not staged. Then, Glenn's booming deep hardy laughter filled our soul, making that moment even better. Albeit I know from decades of Eaglemania dedication that Glenn and Henley liked everything and everyone to follow the script.

To me personally, it was Henley Heaven. He would never forget the Shepherd...it was just Don Henley's direct message to **me**, his chibano, the greatest 'Shepherd' fan!

Yes, one truly self-centered girlie.

Seriously, Don Henley is like one tantalizing tough puzzle. Pieces of the jigsaw mystery. Diverse well-planned shaped, smooth edge, single pieces. Solo units dumped, laid out in a complex clumping mound to sort, consider, analyze, arrange. Portions to join together as one.

An immaculate heaping hodge podge of elements that should eventually come together over time that reflect a proposed image. Yet, he is one puzzle of mystic I'm not sure we'll ever solve, and I think Henley would prefer to be unsolvable.

However, as for music, Henley will most likely always keep a band surrounding him. A studio, the road, another single, another dream, the magic rolls on. Thankfully, for us meek daydreaming fans, it's compressed into his blood!

For, 'after all these years' Don Henley does continues to burn hotter than the Texas sun out there on the back forty in mid-July (sorry, if ya ain't a southerner and why of course, honey, I know you are sorry too-bless your sweet little pea-pickin' heart).

And yes, I admit, I am partial to Henley, probably once again slightly influenced by the rose-tainted glasses but when you're Texas hot, you're just hot and when you're the 'Texas best', you're just 'simply the best.'

Hen is a 'machine', a horse that never quits. There are some musicians that never tire and never stop until they are carried off stage feet first. He is undoubtedly cut from that fabric; bless his heart, again we are grateful.

George Hamilton IV sang a song that spoke of emotions, internal feelings, how good music had been to him and that he had something to speak of that nourished the words of his songs. I always felt that pretty much was a good way to think of Don Henley, Glenn, and the Eagles band and their feelings for music, making, sharing, understanding, and playing music.

Never will Henley be without a song in his soul and we're truly amazed that he is so dedicated. We all keep our eyes open and, on the prize, as we climb aboard and continue to ride the dream woven solo Hen or Eagles train. In, two days, he will add on another year, glad you're still around Henhen, grateful you are still here.

Thus, to put this to rest, with the help of a higher power and Don Henley we are all the weavers of our own realities. Dream on, dream on, even after our dreams come true you still *must* dream on...I hope Henley continue to reinforce our dreams and imaginations for a long, long time.

 # 9: *Henley's Caddo*

Caddo Lake a watershed source
it's bald cypress hang
dripping moss of gray
it's Henley's dear baby
by night or by day.

Decrease the flooding
protecting its land
using his voice
to take the stand
making it better for all of man.

 # 10: *Like No Other Torchbearer*

February 12, 2018

In the year of 2017, Don Henley took us all on quite a journey. One more Olympic gold year, one more stellar note-worthy musical chart-topping year, one more superb year of adventures.

Henley began the year with a kick-off tour at Austin City Limits. Then, took to the open road, yet again for another breath-taking sensational twelve-month review of events.

It may be remembered as the year he received an honorary Skoll award from Oxford. Advancing on, to the Classics, east, west and beyond. Gave a 70th Birthday bash with twenty thousand folks, opened Walden Wood's Visitors Center. * Guided Eagles to the Grand Ole Opry house stage, honored Tom Petty MusiCare POTY with '*Freefallin*', found us a radio station on the Sirius XM channel. He along with couple other E's even received the long anticipated well-deserved ribbon accolade at Kennedy Center Honors.

All of this, while still solo touring with his Cass County band! And as well reorganizing tactically his former band to play various Eagles multi-concert dates.

A Southern gent still going strong. A 'beast of burden' the work animal doing the heavy business, he's one brave, tough legendary 70-year-old non-rolling N rocker musician.

Now, this is just off the top of my head. Of course, there was so much more but not to bore others...just goggle him and the year in review, he won't mind, right!?!?

Henley's a state of the art, classy, rare gem, a true one of a kind.

Moreover, there may be millions of stars in a night sky, but since Glenn has passed, Henley seems to have now become more in line as my north star. The primary Polaris, the one that still stands still while all the others dance and rotate around his fixed point. The constant, the one and only radiant one.

Every concert, every song, each word, every line, every endeavor, each year is evidence and reminders of the reasons why we deeply admire, respect, and appreciate Don Henley, his music, the treasure and the wonder that he bestows.

He continues to rain hotter than a southern warehouse full of exploding firecrackers in the midsummer heat during a Texas hailstorm. And as fans, we continue to be honored and forever grateful.

With this in mind, I work diligently to take every opportunity that develops to remind that Henley is a southern gentleman born and bred. Bless his heart, the sizzling sunny pride of east Texas.

Whereas be that as it may, in the sad year 2016, after the loss of our Glenn we were under the impression the Eagles flame had extinguished forever. That candle had burned long and hard for many decades but had clearly gone out...

You may even say, for some of the band members that candle was burned at both ends. We all pondered was there any wax, flickering spark, or wick length leftover?

Yet, Henley represents a spark, a flame of hope.

The returning of the return.

Yet again, like our own personal Olympic game champion the music flame lighting ceremony rekindled for the Eagles band in 2017. Don Henley worked his magic once more craving the candle wick, igniting the match while his own musical magic travels continues to shine as well.

What a year, what a blast. What a bright glow he cast. (And this is only what I can remember without any Henley personal knowledge or in-depth research, what else, who knows!).

In the same light, I have been pleading for Henley to be around for at least 484 more years to celebrate life, brighten our path, and rock the world. (We all know Joe Walsh will still be around, whew thank goodness Uncle Joe cleaned up his act!).

After all, I am confident if anyone can have that lasting power it is Don Henley. Of course, he's our 2017 gold medal Olympic trophy annual winner, for actually he continues to be a trip like no other.

* Henley's contribution to the ongoing support and legacy of Walden Woods should not be underestimated. While I not a mountain hiker or sweating on the wilderness trek kinda gal I love observation of majestic breathtaking view. But that view and exploration is from the ground. I am grateful for proper conservation of wilderness preservation. Like those unwavering ones before him, Howard Zahniser, Grinnell, Teddy R, John Muir, Henley is devoted to this project, others, and the great American outdoors.

11: *The Spellbinding Patience of Don Henley*
July 29, 2017, Op-Ed

Life can be so good and hold some wonderful events, days, memories. For instance, a few times I have been honored to be part of events that hosted Don Henley private performances, closed tapings, interviews. These occasions include segments where individuals communicate with Henley specific inquires, they had contemplated. Watching and listening to him chat and/or respond is a stunning, intense event in and of itself.

Now, I don't compare one event to the other. I am just grateful the Henley mystic continues. He is an enigma. You just never know with Henley-well you think you know; you think he is like meticulous, calculated, scripted. However, the delightful surprise is you don't always discover what or where he will venture next in his journey.

Thus, I consider each *Henday* a new exciting chapter in a heart-warming well-written book. A new enlighten turn, thoughtfully processed, crisp new page, slightly different concert, a unique set of known and mysterious foretold unfolding, as each time is a dramatic page-turner chapter with D Henley.

During Don Henley experiences, I am fascinated as well by the discussion each has a need to share with Henley. Usually intriguing tidbits. A unique chance to share a few minutes in the sun with one of our greatest spellbinding storytellers.

You cling to the edge of your chair frozen, riveted to his every move, every word, each breath, every pause, his wit, charm, laser focus, his genius. It's purely enthralling. In the seventies, Henley stated he was just like everybody else.

Lord, please.

Nonetheless, remember Equestrians desire and seek the legends. The unique, elegant, the remarkable thoroughbred bloodlines. For they carry 'the proud look' in their eyes-often described as "the look of eagles." Hmm, interesting. Henley appears to carry that legendary mark and the proud eye look.

Not that I'm implying Henley is an animal, quite the contrary. Just using analogy, my skill and keen perspective for picking a champion of the winner's circle.

Yet, (here we go, buckle-up, Negative Nelly Neata in Nylons) on occasion I heard repeated phrase or question that make me wanta roll my eyes and wonder how on earth Henley holds it all together.

Frankly, sometimes I want to speak up or yell, "hey you, haven't you followed him for forty years don't you know this, or do you google?" I have seen seasoned journalist as well ask things that were prior fact, well-documented information, or inquires ya shouldn't be asking. Do your research honey! God bless 'em. Henley handles it all meticulously, of course.

Now, I don't mean to be rude and it's not all prior revealed knowledge. To me it displays wasted time, wasted sentence, or wasted opportunity. However, for each individual experiencing this is a rare moment of treasure-a time to connect. After all, it is the one and only DHenley a valued national treasure!

While there are many tales furnished as recited repeats, they are still compellingly engaging first or fifteenth round. As well there's always new news, ideas, and potentials in the works that are shared. And new fans continue to discover Hen after all this time; so, great.

Each communication diverse, exciting, and interesting. Through it all, it is simply mesmerizing just to watch Henley in action doing one of the many things he does so well and eloquently. Gosh, he probably hates every second-but like with cobra's we are charmed!

Mr. Henley patiently sit there probably apprehensive but replies, diligently addresses each person respectfully, moves on. I have even personally witnessed someone be what I considered downright disrespectful with a statement; he just turned the issue into a positive retort.

OMG, no wonder we adore him!

His patience, his voice, and that rare, rare, rare, rare million-dollar award-winning smile warms our heart. He makes ya just wanta hug him-or is that just a southern gal thang? Speaking, smiling, sharing, singing, still he is humble and stunning.

Personally, I have experienced the honor of meeting many celebs, CEO's, Colonels, Deans, Judges, musicians, factory workers, construction folk, street people, various dignitaries, etc. Maybe it's not smart, but I don't rattle easily.

However, I have met two distinguished gentlemen that totally intimidated the fool out of me. One of them was Christopher Reeves-Superman, surely understandable, it's Superman!

That other one; just a southern east Texas singer in a band. Why would anyone be a flustered moron unable to comprehend thought or form word due to a simple, humble singer? Bless his heart. How did Joe Walsh, Timmy, and others think or sing on that stage with him present?

Henley is powerful, articulate, moving, warm, cool, chatty, quiet, amusing, humble, informed, gifted, calm, conscious, conscience, heartfelt, vivid. He is like an expensive finely crafted bottle of wine; he just gets better and better with age. You think he can't, but he does.

Pure, graceful 'poetry in motion'. All that aside, he is just simply Don Henley. And we are all grateful that he is. Dear God, above, please let him live to be 484 years young!

In essence, if you get *any* opportunity to attend any Henley-related event I strongly encourage you to do so as I can assure you that you will never, never be disappointed.

I am just so grateful for the solace of past memories that I hold from my first moment of the Glenn Frey head lift, to each song, every guitar lick, every chapter, to all patient Don Henley chatting seconds. Life has been good Joe-spellbinding and good. Rock on!

12: *Created 2014 for Christmas Cards*

Merry, Ho! Ho! Ho! Joyous cheer, peace on earth, glad tidings. Heavenly blessings. Good wishes. Healthy healing holidays. Use energy for kindness. Live everyday like it's Christmas. Carry joy and laughter inside and share. Be unique, give of yourself, impact the world with positive spirit. Jingle all the way. Candy canes, Believe! Feed the reindeer, drink the root-beer. Seek a prosperous bright New Year. Bless the baby Jesus, God save the Queen, thank goodness for Glenn Frey & Don Henley...And, whatever else we need to cover to be PC enough to avoid the lawsuits! ~ Anita G Shepherd

13: *Hens a Scholar Quotin' a Scholar*

I worship when Henley
Quotes a verse
Rhythm or reason
Time or season
To listen to him
Roll out the words
Of other scholars
Of long ago
How does he do it
How does he know
Word for word
He quips with ease
Phrases sentences
To the ear they please
Give us more of your
Knowledge and wisdom
Quote some verse
That brings new meaning
Share with us all your
Mind, words, verse, and reasons.

"If a man does not keep pace with his companions, perhaps it is because he hears the
sound of a different drummer."
~(Thoreau)

14: *Don Henley will be 71 Yrs Young!*

July 22, 2018 Birthday

We used to spend our time
flippin' radio stations
as music was
the only love we'd known
but Don Henley released us
from reaching
to change that dial tone
as he brought us back
some good ole Eagles songs.
We looked for harmony
in all of its stages
found slim pick-ins
to the chart's pilin' high
but when he bestowed his soul
no time was a-wasted
'cause there nothing like
a Hen tune
soaring in our sky.

15: Potential contributions submitted pages for 70th Birthday Book for Don Henley July 22, 2017 (NOTE: Unsure if any materials below were included as did not review end results of project).

a) Page 1 Submission:

My response to the question: How you became interested in Don Henley?

When I was 14 years old, I went up the street and babysit three kids. The oldest introduced me to this sassy, bold, rebel singer with this mane of untamed, uninhibited hair-then, I followed the Eagles for 42 years.

Forty-two yrs HenHen how does it go so fast? It was a thousand years ago, but it was only the blink of an eye. It was yesterday but it was not yesterday.

Around 1978ish that singer crushed my little teen spirit when he Michael Boltoned 'our' hair. Granted, at this point in time we had no clue who Bolton was, but Glenn cut 'our' hair...ahhh the good ole days.

When you're 14 you think it's all about being smitten. Then, you slightly mature, life gets more complicated, and you ponder if it was possibly more than hot, sizzling desperado guys & hair. Now, don't get me wrong, we like the hot, we like the sizzle, we adored that hair!

Fans always felt Eagles band and each individual guy just had it right.

Those voices, that talent, the words cut right to the heart of human emotion. In the long run (no pun) the music rose above everything else for it connected with us on some personal level-that touched our lives, rocked our world, grasped onto our emotions.

Then, on January 18th our world was shaken again. I don't know why I was so devastated; I never even knew Glenn Frey. Eagles made the greatest most profound impact on my life of anyone I never met. We are truly, truly sorry for your loss.

I don't know how you find the appropriate means or the right words to say to Don Henley 'thank you' for all you have given us over the last forty-plus years. It is amazing and commendable the influence you make on generations and the world. We are honored and eternally grateful for any of your time, your music, or your life you share with us. As well, humbled by your ongoing dedication to Walden Woods and all its splendor.

So, to answer the question: Sorry Hen, it was Glenn's fault (& maybe GF hair!).

Thank you again Mr. Henley for the Dallas TX birthday bash weekend.

Be well, stay safe, keep taking those powerful vitamins-son, don't know what's in them but they're doing their job! To wrap it up, we'll just 'see you down the road'!

b) Page 2 Submission:

Henley's Silence:
Silence is golden
so Henley said
wonder where silence
is the golden
of rule that he read.
If silence is golden
could we hear
Desperado's song
a golden throat sound
sing through our ear?
The silence of stillness
rings in our heart for
Henley's sidekicks departed
sadly there's no more
Frey words to be said.
The mellow voice
of silence stirs in our head
how can we response
with stained tears shed
flowing bright red?
Silence is golden
so what do we hear
if we close off our
mind and patiently
listen with our ear?

c) Page 3 Submission:

Opposites?
He likes the land, I like the sea
He likes the button-down, I like the Tee
I prefer sky-blue, he'd choose moss green
He lives in the land of Cowboys; Atlanta Braves are my team.

He's a patience loiterer; I'm a dance queen,
He & Joe bond with The Who; but Glenn Frey is my dream.
Silence is Golden he deems,
No! it's highly overrated I confidently scream.

Your correct honey is his genuine theme,
his sparkling blue eyes make us softly beam.
An environmentalist for outdoor scenes,
a delicate Southern flower with seeds extreme.

How do you understand one of such different means?
Well, despite any evident distinction to see
he makes your heart dare to rip open it seams
each time he sings Desperado on stage or in dreams!

d) Page 4 Submission:

"Don Henley I are Not!"
I realize I'm not Don Henley when it comes to the word
I know I missed the talent show
where you reserve
verse or phase upon the stage of great inherent
writing capacity;
it would reveal a tune or stanza
that heeds refrain or flairs a gift
so as with purpose is given too few
who share the world juncture
with fanfare moments
creation to display
while some hold expression that heal,
others sit in the voice audience silent and still.

SECTION FIVE: EAGLES BAND

"Admiration is a feeling that we can't resist. When two different worlds collide,
to enjoy is to smile, for all the right reasons, give, share and sacrifice,
in and of all the right seasons."
~ (Anita G Shepherd)

1: *It's Reigning Men, Hallelujah!*
September 25, 2012, Op Contributor

Rain, rein, reign according to the English dictionary can be described as a noun, verb, or adjective for pouring/falling/shower/season, pulling/control, dominance/prevalent power/period of time for a ruler.

That's wonderful for me as I like to shake things up or more specifically shake words up sometimes. And too often, I just plain twist it all up...not intentionally but sometimes at my hand, speech, or keystroke good words suffer.

Mentally time-traveling recently, I was thinking about this in remembrance that I had documented once some good words about Kurt Russell being the jungle boy of Gilligan's Island in 1965 Season 1, Episode 19. However, in looking back, it's been almost a year since that notation. Where does time fly?

To self-plagiarize, '*who could resist a leopard print outer wear'n loin cloth rocking handsome youth who could swing on a vine and float away in a helium balloon.*' By the way, in sixty-five unlike Jackson Browne I wasn't

21, I was five years old and thought that daytime stood still and that all reined right with the world. Hallelujah!

A few years later, here comes a gorgeous tambourine shaking music man holding a microphone standing on stage singing. OMG, Dave Jones to the rescue. A Manchester pop-rock fellow in a band. He cheered-up this sleepy 'daydream believer!' I didn't think life would ever get any better. A young dude that could swing on a vine and one 'white knight on a steed' that could carry a tune standing on stage.

Then suddenly, there was Glenn Frey.

In a life changing instant Glenn rocked my world totally off its axis. Glenn, just one simple but powerful word. One living word.

That instant awakening is comparable to Helen Keller's descriptive moment for the simple sign language word 'water'. As she ascribed that one word gave her joy, light, freedom, hope and awakened her soul. Just one living word.

Glenn, one word.

Glenn made my heart rain fruit loops, an exhilarating gale force downpour of water. I was all of fourteen by then. Old, mature, knowledgeable, and adding up the far away hotties like a pro.

Now, don't get me wrong I didn't toss away the jungle boy or the Saturday morning tambourine playing DJ, I just rearranged that young teen idol listing. An Eagle, an island guy, and a Monkey, oh child it is raining men. Now that's truly twisting it up!

More important, I knew immediately that 'Glenn' could not only stand on a stage, sing into a mic, play in a band, swing from any vine he desired, toss a head of hair, singe my soul but as well do it while strumming guitar strings-flat top or electric, lord help us all!

And thank you lord-for whatever reason and pleasure that came along...

takes me right back to my twelve-year-old self singing Kris K's' *"Why Me"* (Lord) song in a gospel church group then later with Anthony Carter in school for Glee Club. Great line, great saying, great singer(s).

Incidentally, people seem to love to say the line to me "Glenn may have suck ya in, but you stayed cause of Henhen." They would just be so wrong. Maybe, they just don't know me...hallelujah.

Now, not that I am not a faithful admirer in a whole different method of appreciation of Don Henley. He's an impressive wingman for Glenn Frey. No disrespect intended to my urbane, charming, collected Lonestar Southern country talented brother in spirit from Texas; it's just a holy alternate process in Anita world with 'Glenn'.

When my nephew Hunter was nine, he said to me "Aunt Trouble, you are a stalker." I quickly replied son you do not understand that word. I am just a fan. I have never driven by Glenn's house!

Thank goodness for a time period with no google maps...through I have been a faithful receptor of the Eagles newsletter for decades. But that doesn't validate me as a tracking cult member, right?

In the same light, stalking an obsessive need to pursue prey (oh no way, but he is an eagle, hmm) often unsuspecting prey...hmm...And, that would be a lot of work and frankly I'm kinda lazy. I just consider myself a **'DAD'** (not a daddy, *I a girl*) a dedicated addiction devotee.

So, how can you describe that smitten Glenn Frey plague, virus, the controlling rein to a nine-year-old that don't understand devoted affection, that affinity affiliation, the bonded admiration seal?

Attraction can be a powerful magnetic force. I never held the word gift of Don Henley or Miriam Webster but Lordy, lordy Glenn was so wickedly marvelous-a reigning purely tremendous treasure, hallelujah!

Once you go all in for your dedication pledge to Glenn you never back down. Or, as per Mr. Henley, that notable wordsmith "you can never look back". There will never be another GFrey in my reign of teen journals.

Glenn was to music what Tom Hanks is to a movie screen, what an ivory middle 'c' note is to a piano, a bone is to a dog, thread is to fabric, paint was to Monet, or a dozen roses represent on Valentine's day. Well, maybe he just meant a little more to some aficionados and was way more enjoyable than bones or roses.

I dove headfirst into the Glenn pool, deep end. Yet isn't falling for the stars, the legends, and spirited musicians what is expected of fourteen-year old's?

Now, remember all this was only from afar and with all the best intent, respect, and preaching's of no improper impurity. Which he should probably be grateful to the good lord above for, as well possibly due to a bit of reining fear of my Southern religious daddy at home and that reigning private Christian high school I attended.

Moreover, it's best I think that only God and I knows the actual potential affect and way Glenn shook-up and influenced my teenage timeframe. I felt it from day one, that Glenn had that magnetic rarity spark, that, he's gonna make it-successfully to the top...it charged and danced in the air around him.

That ability to succeed in a place where many are left behind. With a confident drive and purpose, he came to LA in an ole beat-up Chev, carried a flat top, held a million-dollar ambitious spirit, and a golden far-reaching dream. Did I mention that cool swagger, the hair, and that he was so pretty!

But that was another lifetime; long, long ago. There has been a couple of other affable delightful guys since those years added to that reining pile of three adorable hunks, characters like Thomas Sullivan Magnum, Jack Tripper, Jack McFarland, and oh my 'the accidental fireman' Patrick Sullivan (ya know that Morgan dude). Yowzah, how could ya not add them.

There is some pattern here for symbolic role portraying super soul. Or could be because I was once upon a time such a total drama queen, no longer of course. Ok, so I'm being silly creating an imaginary fantasy land. But we know we can't live like that, it's not reality.

Yet, there is only one idol. (Sorry second runners-up, it doesn't mean in any fashion that you weren't appreciated.)

Now reality serves that in girlhood I was smitten with Kurt Russell, infatuated with Davy Jones but idolized to the core Glenn Frey, my destiny. Aww.

Today, I understand that Glenn put the world in perspective, set the right tone, played the right notes. For, he made my heart sing, made my spirit dance, my steps lighter, and my soul right in harmony with the universe. I am not delusional, just human, maybe slightly gullible but believed in dreams.

Lord, my heart rained some strange sentimental fruits about them all but never one like my Glenn. They, me, we all have grown, moved to other roles and look at things and cutie pie fellas in a more wholesome diehard honorable manner. Well, at least we try.

Glenn Frey, Tom Selleck, John Smoltz, Dean Cain, Ann Rule, Uncle Cracker, Casey Kasem, Kid Rock, Bob Seger…who would have ever imaged a southern mild-mannered country girl could experience such zest and thrills from a bunch of Michigan area idols. Solid as rock, like a rock, spinning rock, fever in the heart, top dog, men of steel-no regrets.

As for and by current standard, I still enjoy the twisted list, the down-pouring rain, and handsome guys. I don't enjoy so much when I encounter distasteful grownup misconduct. Being a committed disciplined follower, this strike me as oddly creepy. Freedom of speech-well listen here adult child they are good-hearted daddies now; be respectful.

None the less, I like when people say respectfully, they are sweet, cute, etc. They are, well especially Glenn. It's always interesting when someone voices their selection of admiration for one particular Eagles dude. Then, I ponder wonder why, why they choose this **one**...

And I know Glenn Frey truly remains one pretty thang and I still adore Glenn properly. As we age, maturity serves us in the reality that the body is an outer shell. While we all like that outer to look nice, what we are is identified inside. The inner heart, soul, feelings, spirit.

Of course, it's a whole different rain on the parade when you are five, 14, 29 or when everyone pined or being pinned upon is single. Unsure when you get to the rite of passage or the age of noting your attitude change. Aging doesn't make you blind when you're an oldie it's just feels peculiar-at least to me. But hallelujah to each his own right, for time and change march onward, and it marches fast.

Yet, unable to prevent the rolling flow march, time slips through our fingers like its liquid mercury. Like it's dew evaporating in the hot morning south pole sun.

Even so, again, where has time and the changes gone. How does a lifetime pass so rapidly? How did we learn to adapt to time and accept changes? How did I get so ole and in my head, they still remain reigning young?

One day you're watching a Saturday morning show then in the next couple weeks you're at the late-night Saturday show and it seems like only a few month later you about ready for the end of the reign nursing home's Saturday afternoon early-bird evening show...and yet it was decades and decades.

Hopefully, those memories of a youthful island lad, the Londoner, and the spry rock star will hang in there better than and longer than many of the Saturday shows, some reigns, other reins, some rains, and the twisted shaky joints-bone joints...which you remember you have when it's raining...hallelujah let it rain, let it rein, let it fall, and let it rain, men oh men!

 # 2: *An Eagles Story*

This is their story
they sang some songs
from days of Mushrooms
to Shiloh from home.

This is their story
how it begun
for all those Eagles
that sat on the throne.

This is their story
they had the faith
and each believed
they were heading some place.

This is their story
traveling along
free in a flatbed
wild girls were strong.

This is their story
runnin' an rippin'
creating the legend
making their living.

This is their story
it's not only a song
they play their best
when all got along.

This is their story
but it all went wrong
for 14 years
nobody was home.

This is their story
hell froze over once
they did return, but
not too bad junk.

This is their story
amazing tours they gave
out on the road
we loved 'em long.

This is our story
we got great songs
they were our ticket
we knew we belonged.

3: *Hotel California XM* (November 17, 2017)

Eagles on the radio
well what do you know
we finally have a channel
hallelujah down below.

Rocking with the Eagles
on the Sirius station
now we're rolling 'n shaking
with sheer determination.

Bringing on the music
zest for all the fans
we love to hear 'em singing
tunes of our band.

Set to the HC station
a new Frey in tow
rolling out those classics
we're singing as we go.

Driving down the highway
or listening at home base
we love the Eagles channel
but miss our dear Glenn's face.

Eagles on that radio
Henley, Timmy, Uncle Joe
finally! they have a station!
hallelujah's roll on, hello!

4: *Kansas*
November 12, 2010, Op-Ed

In childhood we were so influenced by Kansas. What was it about Kansas? Dorothy Gale, Toto, those ruby red shoes, Aunty Em, Wyatt Earp, Laura & the Prairie's Little House, Marshall Matt Dillon, Ms. Kitty, Joe Walsh, Hallmark, Amelia Earhart, Mary Ann, Horace Higginbotham (you know Mary Ann's Horner's Corners KS boyfriend. After all those years waiting for his typical girl next door to get rescued from that island he finally gave up, moved on. Probably to another Kansas City small town gal) ...

But why Kansas? Why not Iowa where the corn grows high, Colorado with the snowcapped mounts piled rocky high, Montana where the cowboys ride the ranch under that big blue open sky, Dakota plains and those Black hills, the cowpokes roaming their grassland fields, Texas where rangers rope longhorn steers, or New York City with Times Square, Park Avenue and the many, many people there? Genuine Hallmarks.

Down-home small-town feel? Charm, appeal? Magical enchanting folklore? A nice little slice of America? However, did the place actually matter so much or just the thought process.

In reality, in childhood 'I' was always a little afraid of Kansas. All that rough weather, blinding dust storms, battle scarred outlaws, dreadful derelict bandits, ravishing Rocky Mt locust swarms-that large, devastating relentlessness short-horned grasshopper plague, flying well-dressed winged monkeys that lived in the jungle near Oz, Kansas.

Those flying monk primates alone struck the fear of God in yeah! And Dorothy braving that wicked witch, yet let's face it she was a murderer. Killed that witch dead as a doornail she did...You had to be tough to hang in there with Kansas folk.

Still, the mid-western Sunflower state, breadbasket of America, Great Plains expanse, 'people of the south wind' held its draw. Amelia Earhart, the first fascinating adventurous female to fly solo over the Atlantic Ocean was one of the world's most mysterious inflight Pacific Ocean disappearances; a celebrated USA aviator was Kansas birthed. A female Hallmark.

Their Louisiana Purchase state motto is 'to the stars through difficulties'. Amen! What a powerful statement. The Missouri Territory real estate grounds serves as our nations geographic center.

There're open green landscapes, wetlands, chalk towers, grain fields, salt mines, Eisenhower's brain in Wichita, Wild Bill west show, Fort Leavenworth, Chisholm wagon trail, lots of cattle, lots of banks (rivers and check cashing kind) and the silver rush. Where basketball, air jet assembly lines, and 'get out of Dodge' were invented. Maybe that's why there were so many long-range, precision shooting, repeating firearms carrin' guys that rode out the dust storms, faced frontier gunsmith justice pioneers, cyclones, and wicked witches. Hallmarks?

And don't forget there were many salons with pure whiskey, high-stake card games, and those dance-hall girls that entertained and worked for Ms. Kitty to visit and sit a spell with...(gosh, I'm shocked Joseph Fidler Walsh would leave all that...but at the time I think he was only 'bout two years young-so, oh well, 'oh yeah' possible influential fodder for his indulgent mischievous future-hmm).

Yet, many like the plain, laid-back ordinary, low-key lifestyle. Gentle, carefree safe days, small towns and happy go lucky times. As in childhood we often yearn for and seek the environment of simple.

As Don Henley (high-quality hallmark) detailed "somewhere back there in the dust, that same small town in each of us". Well, it was *The End of the*

Innocence'. Was he truly singing about towns, dust, or simpler days? The end of childhood?

When our "beautiful, for spacious skies" were poisonously tainted by the damaged fairy tales, do we at least mentally search to find a simplistic place to wash our sin? Maybe, maybe not but just "take a long last look" as we watch that "tall grass wave" in the Kansas wind...

Thus, in my basic mental Kansas fairy tale, Mary Ann would have just moved on to the jungle boy aka Kurt Russell! Not Kansas-born but who cares, it's the jungle boy! Hallmark!

Who could resist a leopard print outer wear'n loin cloth rocking handsome youth who could swing on a vine and float away in a helium balloon...and dad-burn-it the jungle boy probably landed in Kansas like other potential balloonist.

Now, I was only five when that balloon lifted off the island but like Walsh maybe I was preparing for those later years and spectacular entertainment. Take one last mental look...ghaaa-rawl lord the jungle boy! Lordy, lordy Toto, we can't be in Kansas anymore!

At least somebody got off that island, me and Goldie are proud. And hopefully jungle Kurt had the opportunity to sit and 'watch the clouds roll by' and odds are most likely he didn't have flying winged jungle chimps as pets.

So, for myself, my red slippers, Dorothy, Toto, Hallmark and maybe Henley, there is no place like home, easy Kansas style, innocence feel of childhood, uncomplicated fairy tales or just simply simple times. No place like home, no place like Kansas, no place like home, no place...

5: *ARR*

I see the band take the stage
feel the heat beat with the souls
stirring tunes giving out swoons
filling our time with soothing grace
sharing their part right from the start
of each word of every stroke
picking the setlist, playing their songs
as we all move, cheer, hum along
to the spirit to belong
to the music that's the goal
to the heart to the soul
of our *American rock and roll.*

 # 6: *Them Eagles*

Rolling country rock outlaws
breaking it all apart
casting aside the fray no easy parts,
tested the limits, bent all rules
push pedal down steady
hard and fast out of school,
anti-authority
cool dudes' attitude
big fools dreamed large
guitar tools for-far up a chart,
into a-many girls enamored
blood-red quivering heart
off the rails, off the track
on the beat, on the heat
in the street
yes, they were indeed
an intense retreat
that steady 2-4 base
of good rock N roll
lives on the heart
of the music's true soul
while one may be gone
his words are still here
ringing loud and proud
those songs play it clear
when we need a memory
that crisp sound still beats
and repeats a melody
oh, so dear and so sweet.

7: *Belief*

Things I believe in:
>   without fail the sun will rise in the East tomorrow,
>   Eagles music will always bring a smile to my face,
>   that long after we are gone, the moon & the stars live on,
>   bedtime prayers bring us some measure of comfort,
>   in the end the only ones you can truly count on are blood-
>   of course, those bloods that chose to love you 'unconditionally',
>   and that real loyalty is found with man's best friend
>   our tail-wagging canine, bless-their-soul, pooches.

8: *After the Classics Then What?*
July 30, 2017, Op-Ed

>   Is this the Eagles last chapter or is it a new begin
>   we are out in the weeds, waiting wondering
>   what do we reach for, are there new fears coming
>   are we all sublime, do we live in the presence
>   with a renewed sense of design
>   Deacon and Gill provide new chimed lines
>   but will it all last, will it all be fine
>   or will they just fly downward in final decline?

With each revision for the band the voices may have sounded slightly different, but the music played on. They continue after decades to remain treasured and in the limelight. Their star hasn't faded, their distinction is still present, harmonies remain dynamic, and their fans remain fateful.

While, progress leads to change, change creates new. Sometimes with change the old slightly fades. I think for many Eagles fans we will always long to have Glenn, Henley, Bernie, and Randy be some part of that new but sadly they will not be able to continue to sing our tunes,

their tunes.

Yet, one pluck of a cord and we were all right back to the flow of the beat. Rocking out. That's the thing with music, a song can impact, carry us through, and move us in ways many methods do not allow.

Glenn was the one that took the first step forward in forming a band. Glenn was the one that hit the pause step. Did Glenn have the final say in the reuniting touring in '94 of the band? *Glenn Frey.*

People were present, then for various reason needed to refocus. So, there was another who came in, to carry-on. People kept the music playing. Thank goodness for the ones present at the time and for the ones who were able to step-in when need arose.

They *always* came back to us. The Eagles came back strong as ever. Maybe because of that perseverance, that drive, focus, talent and maybe because of each one's sincere heart and the love of their music.

So often I would look at things as something was being taken away.

How dare they…I would feel threatened, insecure by their changes and what fans were losing. Perception here not a fortune telling prophet, could we "learn to live without" them? Oh, what a hollow thought. The "shadows would come to stay."

Shamefully, I focused on the negative, instead of being grateful for the positives. Thankfully, they knew, and overtime realized what was significant. Clairvoyants?

In effect, even though, the voices may have altered, the tunes for some of the most outstanding unforgettable songs we get to hear do play on. So, whether they continue together or walk off our stage, we still have their songs to carry us forward.

Isn't that what we need?

9: *More Eagles thoughts…*

All around we have our intense hobbies
sometimes they come and go in phases
or overtime they last for many ages
some collect salt & pepper shakers
sculpt wet dry clay night and day
learn a foreign new language skill
take cooking classes with the masses
paint elaborate images that chill
travel and sightsee for a thrill
garden with style by the yard
tinker with piano tunes that swoon
gather lighting' bugs by the light of the moon
are diehard deadheads some would be parrot heads
but as for me and mine we would be
Eagle heads and that's just plain
simply divine and quite a-ok all right & fine.

10: *Eagles: SDD-sinfully delicious desperado's**

(*Debated titling this: 'Boy Scout Vices', 'Don Henley is Killing Me!' 'Old & New Classics', or SDD-so later you as the reader can make your own pick)
October 23, 2017, Op Contributor

Good music is like cranking up a vintage sports car. Makes you one pure sassy hellcat bad gal. Bravely opening the door, sliding onto the distinct slick leather seat, putting the key in the ignition, firing that baby up, stepping on the gas pedal. Ah, sweet heaven. Listening to the engine roar to life, purring as it speaks to you "hey sassy cat, turn that radio up above the standard ear-splitting vibration position, drive me down the road, shift into gear, be alive, let's go honey. Gun it!"

Now, that's just the way Eagles tunes make ya feel; cranked up, in gear, alive, and gunning it down some road. Those sinfully delicious desperado dudes were always singing about cars, roads, fast lanes, women, highways, being high on the wing, feeling alive. From the first electrifying song you are hooked. The beginning a cappella notes of "…stars in the Southern sky" all the way to bringing it home with "before it's too late". It makes and keeps us in step, happy, enthralled and filled with goosebumps yearning for more of the old, the new, the classic.

Fortunately, God blessed me with three gifts, a witchy attitude, a hearty appetite, & Eagles band. What more could a woman need? We're the generation that got the Eagles! Yes, they have somewhat crossed into younger gens, but those kids don't know how to appreciate what we got to experience long ago with the band. Sheer heaven.

That Eagles band is winding down the highways still today, in their own fast lane playing and singing tunes. Currently departed Seattle, Greensboro, Atlanta, winging their way to Kentucky entourage in tow, Detroit & Nashville Opry upcoming. Papa Hen leading the charge, with Walsh, Timmy, VGill and Deacon Frey (aka Teen Jesus) sharing the spotlight. But sadly, for me, searching the rear-view, no Glenn Frey to the stage floor plan.

Over decades, we observed, grew, improved, expanded, and evolved our own life in yearning immolated fashion. Even more, I think for some of us we like to remember the outstanding music, the harmonies, the way all those E guys made us feel good and tuned in to their world, their soul, their rhythm.

While 'Eagles' today may not be exactly like the band we remember of the past, they are still making and playing those outstanding music tunes. And, as well putting together one great concert show after another.

Today, I just focus on those goodies, the good things, good reminders, the good feels, good music and all the happy notes they placed in my heart. Like the art of Japanese Kintsugi, we embrace any of their potential damaged flaws with solid gold solutions. As we all hold flawed cracks in our history.

Of course, we know somewhere back there in our recess there were things rattling chains but, perhaps it's best to let those prisoners stay in silent locked solitaire.

And hey, as E fans, we never expected choir boys.

Yet, wait there's a but...always a but, an oh if only coming...Yet, But, whatever-there are a couple of things currently that slightly concern me more than flaws or another missing Eagle from the stage line-up. Missing meaning for me, no Glenn, no Randy, and the lack of Bernie. Those of the past. The absent.

Maybe it's shouldn't be what's a missing void but what can be added to enrich. And, so be it not my call for who is permitted to stand on stage. But one of much greater power and far, far wiser knowledge determines that arrangement for us. Of course, they know the band the best.

Provided that, first concern, are we enjoying the gift of the moment? Concentrating? Focusing. That's why Henley instructs put down that phone and soak in the now.

We are all living life way too fast in the rapidest forward moving lane with so many of our radio hero singers going forever silence, moving out of our rearview mirror and flying home. Radio knobs that have been flipped into the permanent off slot. I realize that's life but it's just sad.

Second worry, Don Henley.

Yes, again Mr. Henley.

He is finally going to kill me. He is honestly going to make me have a bonafided stop-my -heart, mid-musical beat heart attack. A massive acute coronary, I feel the arrhythmia's building. He is pushing me over the borderline that will surely finish me off.

Well, why you may wonder? Because Henley is still jumping on stage. I mean literally jump-bouncing up and down on stage!

Stop it now Henhen.

I know he's always had the tendency to like the jump, but Jesus, son, you are seventy and a grandpapa. Has the butter slid off his biscuit? We know you love to rock but let the 24-year-old guy do your jumping. You are not Van Halen; you are petrifying us.

I am thinking lord I am going to have to do CPR on Don Henley. No Neonatal ICU nurse on this green planet wants to resuscitate an adult. We love you and need you to stay young for a long, long, long time; please no jumping-not even with your General Practitioners permission!

Besides I think jumping on stage during rock 'n' roll is one of the South's seven deadly sins...what are we gonna do with him.

We got that sinful desperado, Joe Walsh, straightened out now Hen's trying to give us heart failure. There never seems to be a dull moment for the E team.

But why stress, oh well there's nothing I can do about either, so I just crank up the CD (DVD or cassette-oh yeah still got 'em) and listen to any or all of them do what they do best-sing, write, create incredible music. Our desperado's, rolling on, still flying.

All the same, it's admirable and amazing the Eagles continue to rock and roll onward. They have continued to return, resurrect, revise and survive. What matters most is that they still continue standing, still harmonizing, still on our stages giving it their all, still yearning to and still soaring high and strong.

Still in our hearts. While those Hollywood director Brothers whose film character proclaimed distaste for the band, fans still love 'em. For the average E fan, the members of this band are our musical rock stars.

Eagles, those premiere classic sport models, thrust into the drive gear position. They just keep humming, jumping, purring, and rolling on down our musical highways. Sleek hot rods that for decades stopped us, accelerated, transported, halted, revved, tarred, left their mark on our tracks.

Hopefully, firing it up, roaring and gunning it for the long haul. No need for bad cat stage performers, there will be plenty of those in attendance in the audience. Push the fastlane desperado's, roll on, rock on!

11: *Transformation: Yes, Deacon Frey, We Do Miss Your Daddy!*
July 15, 2017: Break-out Date for Deacon's First E Stage Appearance @ Dodgers Stadium

Deacon Frey is now on the scene
he makes us all young, shout, & scream
just like daddy long ago singing song
with the beat of the greatest band around
and all the fans up to their feet
here we go in the same chord
yet with a different Frey now on board
we will follow, give him support and
love him much, watch him shoot up
the record charts and he will know
that deep inside we all feel the
Glenn Frey magic down in our hearts
he surrounds our soul stills soars nearby
through he now lives in Eagles sky
but never forget Glenn, we never will
his spirit's here yet his soul is still,
but his son carries on, toward music fame
and blended harmonies with a killer gang
he calls them uncle and they will stay
close to his protection along the way
carving his path and picking up
running with the band and oh so much
now his search his voice soothes so mellow
soon power reins and he will hear
of more good gains, song and such
will flood our souls and he will
continue to fill dreams and goals
but never gone from our thoughts
is daddy dear and what we hear
or what we former heard when Glenn
was in gear and landed here,
but now we turn to son and friends
they all will plow a brave path again
and lead us on cause Glenn's gone home.

12: *The HIM book*

> Henley, Iheart (aka Glenn Frey) Meisner and Bern
> the HIMs of music life, wickedly hot desperados
> improving our style, driving us wild
> talented genius stars from on high
> cowboys beguiling playing those bars
> with themes of the heart
> on the radio dial
> focused direction for dreams by the mile
> magical spell captivating their power
> rocking our world climbing the tower
> with hit after hit hour by hour
> destination unknown zone
> but with chilling drive
> and a yearn to devour.

13: *Eagles: Opening, Turning, Closing a Page*

December 5, 2017, Op Contributor

Like a riveting good book, one that grabs ya from the first words, Mr. Glenn Frey sucked me straight into the Frey web. What a moment in time. I was smitten in an instance, entranced, trapped but thrilled to be...history-making memory for a good book that is burned into forever.

As for good books, I wondered for decades why they didn't write a book. I wanted to shout hey Henley we need a book doggone it! I did hear several band members state they had considered. And I read couple books, tons of articles, blogs etc re: E's that were illuminating, vicious, exciting. Right or wrong, agree with writer or not they fuel our resource energy need.

The band's lives were an open yet closed book. Many paragraphs were revealed overtime on the guys, many were never shared, and many more chapters I'm sure could be documented. Regardless, I do think this is some of their appeal-the unknown.

The mystic, the rush of that hold your breath you will never know or anticipate what comes next despite repetition and perfectionism at its best. I basically love hearing E news, but I also appreciate the fact that they all seem to hold on to elements that are uncharted, personal, private, loyal, and respected.

Now back in the day, I became a self-declared teenage Glenn Frey expert historian. This proclaimed title gave me undeserved privilege to the band's decision-making skill (ha!). Thus, I had no problem arguing (in my head and from a far distance) with Henley or Glenn and their decisions. I still don't understand why they couldn't decipher my mental thought process and see that I needed a book penned by them, sharing their personal view. Hmm, a page turner no doubt.

Besides, when I look back over snapshots or videos from the early begins, they all were so smiley and happy. For some reason, rapidly those images changed appearance. Frowns or frozen stares were apparent. Living the American champagne dream, selling huge hit records, having the girls faint at their feet, flying on their private plane, buying anything "dirt to dollars" ...it makes me sad to see those excited sunny faces change.

Man, as an unassuming storyteller and book enthusiast, I always thought I would love to read Bernie Leadon's tale. How has he remained so quiet for all these decades? Joe Walsh said, *"You either gotta rock or be great at the quiet stuff."* Bernie has mastered that quiet stuff. Or maybe he has a gag clause order in his iron-clad E contract that prohibits.

It's ironic that Bernie doesn't get enough praise for his talents. When the Eagles began their innovative incarnation flight, he held the most recognizable name. As a music veteran and stringed-instrumental mastermind he had worked with various well-respected and some of the best country rock bands in music.

Case point, he toiled alongside Flying Burrito Brothers, Linda Ronstadt, David Crosby, Hearts and Flowers, Scottsville Squirrel Barkers, Dillard and Clark.

But what would his view share, what would he have to state? Bernie since specified "*it was my choice to leave when I did. I did it for good reasons, and do not regret it.*"

He always seemed humbly reverent of his departure from the E band and never bomb-basted his former bandmates that I know of. Yet, why wasn't he allowed to sing any solo work-he had great songs, a stunning voice, exceptional talent and why, why, why is he ___not___ on stage as an Eagle? Why?

"*'This isn't the end'. Then he (Glenn) gave me another hug, and we…did the encores and then took our bows together. His statement I took to mean he was leaving it open that I might participate in some Eagles-related event in the future, which I appreciated, and remained open…*" (Bernie Leadon, Jan 23, 2016 regarding: last Eagles concert 2015 July 29 in Bossier City, Louisiana).

Is Don Henley patient with him, does Henley even like him or vice versa… Randy's a whole other crate of oranges. (Randy like Bern also had some pretty impressive art associations before 1971). Now, I hold the highest regards for Don Henley and mean absolutely no disrespect, just an honest ponderance.

When I think of Bernie Leadon's remarkable voice especially on the songs "I Wish You Peace", "The Sparrow", "Bitter Creek", "What Do I Own", or "My Man". Each are a soothing thrill. Can't help but wonder if Henley still thinks IWYP is just "smarmy cocktail lounge music" or if he would like to change that comment? Probably not…and maybe that was just hearsay.

Indeed, I think we wouldn't hold so many questions especially regarding Bernie if we had an explanation of his current absence. Just share something with us even if it's richly sugar-coated. Nip it in the bud, put it to rest. Henley is a brilliant expert at making situations positive. Diehards just yearn for a simple answer. I guess I should move past that at this point in time.

Above all, like Bernie Leadon's silence, sometimes silence *is* the best measure, for silence can speak volumes. Like a music measure rest. That symbol of interval space is as critical and necessary as the notes themselves. So, maybe like Bernie I should learn to be more silent on certain topics.

I have no idea what Bernie's silence communicates, but *so what*; when he has chatted during his post Eagles days, he's always respectful. I admire him not just for his outstanding voice and expert musical gifts but for his uncompromising discretion, his ongoing creativity, and his unyielding unfaltering honor. His classy rest symbol, a best seller, mystery section no doubt.

Bernie Leadon wrote "My Man"
it was a song for a friend's embrace
a traditional pioneering country lovin' brother
we miss his presence, his face, his play
we miss Bernie's style, we miss his space
I wish there had been a restored way
for all to get along somewhat a little better
as Bernie said he sang for the people
he stood on the stage right in his place
we wish him peace and amazing grace.

For now, Bernie and Randy seem content, gracious, and grateful. To my knowledge if bitter, don't state concern. Now, both seemed indebted to fans and have bright views; illustrated in interviews, Randy of how much he "appreciated... fans and that is what makes us...it's like a dream...amazing...(fans) makes you feel good". Once, Bernie gently said *"Be nice to one another, it doesn't cost anything, and it makes the day so much more pleasant. Don't you think?"*

Love it! No wonder fans went from idolizing long haired twenty-yearish rockers to realizing what truly matters. Hair; now I think why as teens was hair so important. Long-haired hip-swinging sashaying' singers, Jesus help us all. Still, I think it's been overlooked, under-appreciated, and never been given significant proper credit, those immense treasured talents of Randy and Bernie.

Moreover, if memory serves, Bern and Randy were front men in the begin, with Henley and Glenn as foreground backups. Gosh, what amazing, incredible, polarizing vocals they all shared.

The diverse talent and skills of all the E's is understood. Trend setters from those vocals, the songwriting abilities, master crafters of instruments, that focused passionate attention to detail, to all the elements for making the music happen. Even so, those first four originals were quite a consummate electrifying quartet.

Nobody's voices compare to those four's harmony. Nobody's. That's my perspective you can have your own opinion and idea. They each and together hold many proud accomplishments and tangible awards and possibly a few regrets but that is living and learnings of life.

Glenn on one occasion, discussed that behind closed doors and in the shadows, it's was a dark wild ride. And, if everyone seemed extremely happy and having such fun in the earliest days, how did it all fall so far asunder?

Maybe there really was a 'Commandment rules list' that couldn't be broken. Did they pay a huge price with internal personal relationships for their chance at professional reward? I try not to over-analysis, get too bogged down in those weeds and probably compartmentalize way more in Eagleland than I should.

Yet, I just clung to the way that music carried us through our own learnings of life.

Of course, 'everybody knows' about the band's decades of conflict. From

Glenn's Armageddon notation which most likely prompted Henley's elicit comment for Hell freezing.

In reality, they faced tough decisions; they weren't finished. Glenn commented *"the definition of greatness is the ability to turn a scary situation into something...self-satisfying"* and they did. There would be more chapters to write.

So, despite the turmoil, the friction, the separate separations, the gnashing of teeth, the family eventually grew up, realized and appreciated what they had together as a team, worked through, overcome apprehension and of course went on to soar higher and thrive for several more decades.

Thus, understanding this, my humble assertion for Bern's current silence is probably out of deep loyalty for Glenn and because those Eagles men were family. That united musical family band of brothers was where it all came together; they made the magic happened.

For, at the end of the day, it's about respect and family.

Then, aside from any of that, there's the historical archives, DVD's, and documentary. RockOmemory? (Or Glenn's 'Flat Bed Ford to the Dark Side'). This gave us perspective, well-crafted insight especially on Glenn and means so much now to all the devoted fan base the Eagles accumulated over the years.

Another updated documentary would be nice-the third act, what happens after, however at this point I don't feel that will develop.

In the begin there was Henley and Frey, what a combo. Glenn always like to be near a course (golfin'), HenHen liked to be near a chorus (singin')! I forget that we have busy active lives; we're "busy being fabulous" and pushing our lives "in the fast lane". Besides, maybe some don't love the band or Henley and Glenn probably as much as I did/do, and that too there are many who fly outside the Eagle nest or that they are newbies to the E and their history.

As well, that maybe not everyone understands the Henley heaven humility or the Frey trance. Moreover, I know that by far I am not the only or expert fan that I think in my heart I am, my head reminds me that I don't know all either.

Maybe that's why I yearned for so long for their tactile book, to hold their words in my hand.

Switching gears of another thought, I am unclear why there are individuals in our mist that we feel so awed by, *think we know all about*, or ones we yearn to place on pedestals.

Nevertheless, in my book Eagles won the right to their pedestals.

Still, I've learned as a loyal Henley admirer that he will, can, and does change his mind-thank goodness for his flexibility so there's still some glimmer of hope for his booked articulate account...possibly even a Joe Walsh 'I SURVIVED hell to heaven: my life my story'...but maybe some of those tales should be left in the dust...Shocking Uncle Joe seems to remember so much of those years. How son how?

Yet, today, I could care less if they pen books. Really, I probably rather they don't write. I am more inclined to feel maybe an auto-bio book wouldn't be a good idea.

"There are things of which I may not speak; there are dreams that cannot die; there are thoughts that make the strong heart weak, and bring a pallor into the cheek, and a mist before the eye." (Henry Wadsworth Longfellow, 'My Lost Youth", 1855).

Most of us that have followed the E's long-term know things we probably wish we didn't know or suspect. However, if anyone does a book I, of course, would have to have a copy-preferably a signed one please.

Now, before this book's paragraph closes, I just want 'em to do what they do best while they can-Be Eagles; keep making thrills, keep providing memory making moments, and keep making history on whatever page that opens.

#14: *Glenn Frey's Eagles*

Eagles were such an amazing band
an eminence hit about the lands
their rockin' diverse musical shows showed
and it was astounding that they could create
magic resounding from a pen, paper, arrange a tune
courage shot straight out of a top hat clearly no spin
but it might be a mental sin the levels some fans
drove to in their head with these fine sturdy mellow young men.
Singing from their stools
they held the command
and gave to the audience
one staged illustration by demand
their lyrical range so planned for all on hand
as amazing sounds soar from town to town
they hop and play from their tour dates for devotees
sit positioned 'no yackers, no loitering' can they ever stand.
But one is now gone, and our hearts are heavy
he drove to LA in a beat-up ole Chevy,
Gladys her name
his talent and fame were on the horizon
with a shattering beat pounded the street
and boy were we glad when the hits they did jive
fortunate for boomers to hear those songs zooming
slow steady desperados gave us music complete.
Those emotional highs
those guys those songs
will live long for our true team
we will continue to play them loud, super strong
and with a broad proud beam
for in our hearts we still sing and hear
the rhythmic harmony sounds Eagles gave us so clear
which will go on ringing for many more years.

#15: *The Time Factor*

March 20, 2016, Op-ed

In life, time is an element we all seek, endure, need and are often extremely short on. We search for ways to reprogram time at different ages, different methods, different stages. To clarify, different situations direct us to describe the word time in varied means.

When we are young, we can't wait for the time moments such as first step, first word, time to start school, time to open the presents, blow out the candles and eat cake. We yearn a whole year for Santa and the reindeer's, we can't wait for mama too have that baby and when she finally does it seems forever before they arrive home. (Then, there are the times and situations we want mama to take that screaming baby back to the stork!).

And, we crave deeply for the time to be a teen, long and hard we ache for that time to be able to drive. To learn to drive, to obtain that permit, the real document that officially allows us on the open road with all the big adults, the flatbed pickups and the 18-wheeled two-ton rigs.

Of course, so many other time things we anticipate and can't wait for-the time of graduation, first smooch, a new job, a date, concert, the first foreign trip, marriage, a shiny automobile, that cruise, etc. As kids, we think time is so slow, why do these things have to take sooooo long?

Meanwhile, sometimes, time change happens internally. We feel time, cling to time, we never want to let time slip away, never wanta waste time, never have enough. It's a part of us, somewhere deep down in our soul.

Far to suddenly, we are perhaps thirty and don't wanta be, on account of, we need more time to remain young. In contrast, at maybe thirty, we don't even get the real meaning of time.

None the less, when do we realize that yikes, we aren't younger anymore.

We aren't oldies per say yet, but not considered a spire youthful one with all that leisure time on our hands.

For then, we ponder what has happen to time, where did all that time go.

Time that enemy. The thing that causes youthful adventures to take twice as long. It can capture the moment. How did we let it pass so rapidly?

Why is it ticking? Tick, tick, tick.

Always ticking away much too quickly. Since don't think I ever quipped anything much before of Don Henley (yeah, right) .... but the man is right about time-only a few summers and just brief few springs.

But let it be, for the clock ticks onward. The college clock ticks, baby clock is ticking, the menopause change is coming, the retirement clock ticks ticking, ticking, ticking.

Why can't we hold on to time physically like it's a book? A book we purchased. But time, is more like loaned library material that we retrieved for a brief period and suddenly realize that it must be returned tomorrow because your borrowing leased frame is winding down.

By all means, as we mature the aging factor of life really bring forth a vast impact, an appreciation an emphasis on the word time. And understanding that it's one of those elements we known counts down beyond our control. *"Time, time, ticking, ticking..."* (DHenley).

Shifting sands of time. When the wind blows, changes direction, the sand, the time moves, reforms and we can never move it back.

Thus, time could be described essentially as a molten mercury metaphor. If you were able to hold it in your hand it would simply and quickly drip right off your fingertips and roll away...sadly much in the way it often does in real life.

16: *A few Eagles Spot-points*

In '71 four desperados began, many diverse decades of fun
by '75 *"Lying Eyes"* held Grammy title the first one won.

In 1980, suddenly they went out at their peak but
in '94, they roared back through Hell's frozen heat.

Some Eagles wanted to spread their wings
so flying solo was their desired scene.

Randy & Bern contributed great zest
we love 'em dearly, yes their two of the best.

In '88 Glenn searched his soul found some peace
found some love, tarnish, and gold.

He went away but he never completely forsakes
he returned to Eagles and that's where he stayed.

1998 Hall of fame celebrated inductees arose
where seven spirits sang, spoke, and posed.

In 2016, they took a stint for the grief
in 2017, gladly they returned yet again to repeat.

As fans begged for more of their cool beats
they gave a brief festival for the Classics so sweet.

For 2018, they're bound for the tour bus once more
with a legacy of songs, couple new guitars on board.

Traveling around from town to town
like Glenn Frey before they'll *"Partytown"* on down.

Sharing treasured music, we all long to soak in
we'll yell the sound Henley 'wash away this sin'.

But now what can we expect what will we see
what will become of the remaining three?

They focused their need for our pleads
yet when their voices are silence will that be defeat?

Hell froze over, and it sure seemed brief
as they rock 'n rolled us coolly down to easy street.

Will they make their last stand as the Eagle lands
well we just don't know so we roll on with the band.

17: *A Committed Jivin' Joe Walsh Freak*
October 6, 2012, Op-Ed

I always thought one day I need to say thank you and plead forgiveness to Joe Walsh.

Joe Walsh became an Eagle in the mid-seventies. I was fifteen years immature at that time, but I swear I thought, "What, Joe Walsh, no, no, no!" How dare Joe push Bernie out of the nest.

Well, I'll just have to put Glenn Frey over my knee. Back then, that thought probably would have put a smile on Glenn or Joe's face. Back then...oh lordy, I had so many faults and aftershocks I needed a full-time seismologist on staff (but now I am cured and quake-proof, oh lordy).

Joe was birthed Joseph Fidler on November 20, 1947. I tell everyone that will listen he was born in Kansas, Wichita Kansas. Folk argue with me about this so maybe I have this fact wrong. But, until JWalsh calls and corrects, this is my tune and I'm gonna stick with playing it...I never worry at all now that he would put me over his knee...

The first couple of bands Joe was in were Nomads and The Measles. Of course, the restless wondering traveling freely wildman's first bands were associates of itchy loose as a cannon, red-spotted rapidly spreading measles. A perfect fit! I never see a slide, a talk box, a kid with measles, or a brick pantsuit that I don't say "hey where's Joe, oh yeah, how ya' doin?"

By the way, Walsh is greatly admired by some of the best in the business of rock 'n' roll Jimmy Page; Pete Townshend, Joe Vitale, Eric Clapton, Gregg Allman, his own brother-n-law Ringo Star recognize him for his impeccable skill with guitars. Joe has been described as "lighting in a bottle", a perfect delineation. By the way, I have heard Joe state he was taught to play slide and given his first slide by Gregg's brother Duane/Skydog, an outstanding musician. Using an empty medicine bottle this slide wizard was undoubtedly as well a great teacher, whom we lost way to young in life due to a dreadful unfortunate accident in Macon, Georgia.

As for tragedy accident's, one thing Joe doesn't seem to talk about is his first daughter, Emma. Emma passed away from injuries sustained in an automobile crash on her way to nursery school in 1974 at the age of three.

How do you accept, escape, come to terms with destructive unimaginable trauma? Personal internal war. Regain traction following permanent displacement?

God, no wonder the man drank. That's an understandable reason. How are you supposed to recover from the loss of a child, a tender innocent young child no doubt?

In Emma Kristen Walsh's honor and memory, Joe created his album "*So What*". On the album is a goodbye opus he wrote "*Song for Emma*". He said this song helped him find closure and a way to move past the grief after Emma's passing. And, as well Joe had a memorial fountain placed in Boulder Colorado's

North Boulder Park where she had played as a youngster.

If I had a happiness vessel list, this memorial fountain would be one of the top places listed. It could be my peace offering site to convey my thoughts of thanks to Joe. For now, feeble attempt this is, it will have to suffice.

Remember as well, in another preceding tragic twist of fate, Walsh was briefly a student at Kent State. He has mentioned he was visiting the campus at the time of the historic National Guard showdown. Again, not to support his habit but no wonder the kid needed a drink; or forty!

Later, in 1980, bandanna Joe had a mock-presidential campaign; his platform being "Free Gas for Everybody" and in '92 ran a VP slogan with "We Want Our Money Back!" He even had a campaign song (oh, yeah!). Joe Walsh a political figure, go figure...

Today, when Joe delivers a few chords of "Life's Been Good" people go bananas and they are not seeking their money back. It is a great song and btw sorry, I didn't **email** you Joe, but life is truly good, and you are right, Glenn was great!

Joe Walsh that "CEO clown prince of rock" has been married several times but seems to have finally found his niche and path to family and happiness. Besides, my personal fav Joe song(s) are *"Family"* (& "One Day at a Time") about his family, getting by day to day, and his personal life. You should have this recording, it's pure gold; it's on his solo album *"Analog Man"* along with other great tunes (no, sadly Joseph's not feeding me royalties and hopefully praying for no lawsuit for all his titles notations).

Today, Eagles along with their fruity basket playing tune maker Joe Walsh are and will always remain the best-selling twentieth century American popular music band in history. They are considered to be one of the greatest contributors to country rock music and one of the most influential bands from the 70's.

Joe's humorous creative funny bone, his tremendous talent, his priceless facial expressions, and fluid-liquid-flowing-zany-wacko style with musical instruments have long made him one of the leading guitar players and rewarding stage acts in the world. How Don Henley can stand on stage with Walsh's facial expressions and remain stoic defies me. Guess that speaks to both of their unsurpassed talents.

By the same token, can you imagine *"Hotel Cally"*, *"Life In-Fast Lane"*, *"Dirty Laundry"'* without that jiving Joe tooling around on a guitar neck or *"Rocky Mountain Way"* without a talk-box! Just a wisecrack, but Bee Gee's may have crafted *"Jive Talkin"* not for a movie but about Joe and his squawk box...hmm.

Be that as it may not, as well as fruit-baskets, guitars, talk box, keyboard, trombone, Joe plays many diverse musical instruments including reports that he may play the bagpipes. Hmm bagpipes? Don't remember seeing him bagpiping...doesn't mean he doesn't...internet fact checker need? ('cause if it's on the net...).

And, the fruit basket's a joke, but if you give him one, I am confident he would play it! Aren't you? Look what the man did with a talk box. I can visualize a tour in the making, Joe Walsh and his Fruit Basket Turnovers...

Mae West famously celebrated that basically life only gives you one chance, so work it right and that one change will be enough. Joe Walsh got it; he took her words literally to heart and worked mischievous bewitching shenanigans well, tootling a bagpipe or not.

He's flamboyant but he's not trying to be. Walsh's unrestrained facial expressions are practically indescribable. I stop and consider what wording in our English holds the correct describe but words fail to justify.

He is one great unparalleled laid-back escapade on stage. He's just an adventure that could make the seas churn, the birds take flight from trees, easily and happily rise screaming fans with his steel string licks from their seats. But, is the man-child seizing, thinking, straining, plucking, stretching, constipated, enjoying...?

He is a delightful jester that must believe laughter is the chicken stock made for the soul. Many super-groups have that one hot blonde standout. Eagles fans categorically have a hot blonde matchless rare bird of a different feather. Perhaps, the best way to describe stage-Joe's 'tre-*men*-dous baloney' is near insanity, goofy charm with a dose of magnetic intellectual main show charisma.

Equally, he is plainly as enduring during special media performing spots with interviews, television, or radio. And, my goodness he *'knows what you're doin'* and when the *'storms (a)brewin'''*.

I don't know *how* it happened. I don't know *when* it happened.

But, somehow, I recognized how much I appreciated, adored, and was committed to Uncle Joe! Don't know why but for decades I have called Walsh 'Uncle Joe'... it just seems the right fit for him. You know everybody has an Uncle Joe, at least in spirit and personality.

And, what a performer, what a crack-up, what a class act. He is just one good mood alternating psychedelic, purely natural hallucinogenic wonder agent for the system.

Abruptly, I realized the bitter-pill Joe drug had worn off and I was a wholehearted convert! Might be the possibility for bagpipes, might be slight maturity beginning to kick-in, might be fruit basket playing potential.

Doesn't matter, he loves being high-wattage electric whirlwind gutsy Joe Walsh and we love it too, well **'now'** I-we all love it!

"Everybody's so different-But he hasn't changed" (JWalsh, not direct quote but no less a great song). And, he has changed, still he hasn't changed; only

improved, mended, rehabbed, abstained, survived. He's still Uncle Joe! It's strange the way we change over time and don't even realize. (Another life lesson taught to the hard-minded redhead Southern gal). *

I hope it is obvious that I have come a long way baby through my nasty Walsh phases. For some reason, maybe it was the absence need for Bernie; I had a very difficult time accepting Joe as an Eagles. Like my petty pathetic opine mattered! Jeez, LuWeeez.

So, maybe, one day he will forgive me for being such a stubborn cold-hearted WitchApaloosa and having such disdain for so long for him that I am embarrassed to even remember. And, due to my control eccentric non-drug use fear I should be able to remember yesteryear better, but I cannot, how can Joe?

In like manner, I hear him sometimes say he is embarrassed that he was a struggling addict and that he is not proud of it. Well, that makes me and Joe a party of two. For this purpose, I am also ashamed of my past, my deep dislike of Uncle Joe.

I appreciate you for that humble expression JFW, but don't be embarrassed, we are just grateful you survived! *"The nature of rock and roll: doing too much too young. There is a self-destructive period you go through...lot of people in our business didn't make it. We count ourselves fortunate to have survived"* (per Don Henley). Henley is right, Mr. Walsh, you survived. We are honored to be fans; you are our prescription for brave vigorous free-form courage.

On another positive side, Joe kicked the empty liquid liquor bottles of courage (probably thanked them for their service) and has been sober since mid-90's; one respectable commitment for a rock musician. That makes Joe a loser and a winner. However, I have not meliorated, I am still a chilly Witch, maybe just not quite as cold-hearted.

Now, I am not saying he should wear his habitual addictive crisis like it's a gold badge, it's just a part of his past and he can't really erase it. Did he, like many of us, make mistakes as he was growing up **(is he an adult now, is he 'sane' now, ha, "oh yeah"?!?!)**. At least, he was not a heifer witch about it. Again, we are just profoundly grateful; "Oh, yeah"!

Joe said in an interview that one of his few regrets was not taking a risk to contact Ray Charles and that instead of waiting he should have just said "Hey Ray, I'm coming over". (BTW, Henley stated during Sirius XM days, Ray Charles is his favorite singer. Remarkably, I never forget things like this the Hen or Glenn state). Maybe in some measure, me and Joe have really grown for as he has convalesced, proceeded to heal, shook off his regret, grabbed his talk-box, Vox amp, and Les Paul, he has continued to entertain us far beyond expectation.

Now, I hear the first step in obtaining potential recovery and forgiveness is open admission, therefore, like Joe's Ray Charles moment, instead of waiting, this is my formal Non-regrettable Risk Contact mode: "So hello Joe; how ya doin', I am a poorly recovering ex-JW consecrated 'so what' witch..."

Yet sincerely, and most important, thank you Joe for hanging in there *for me* through hostile tainted bias years, *with m*e during deep hatred of your party-hardy-Warrior-Joe loves him a chainsaw phase, *by m*e for my misunderstanding of what a great twisty-faced, voice box making music man actually can provide, and for all the decades of fun and laughter you gave music fans worldwide, who needed a cure and were seeking a fix.

Joe Walsh is like a spinning top toy. You wind the string and toss never knowing where that object will land, how long it will spin, or what show will be displayed. But you know, if you let it play out on it's on accord, it's uncontrollable, exciting, fun and one colorful splendor.

For these reasons, let me just wrap by simply decreeing, I am one thankful, eternally committed "tre-*men*-dous" Joe Walsh fan. He's jivin' cool Joe, oh yeah; Amen.

*Today, in one of my prized Eagles keepsakes shadow boxes there is a humble photo from Joe's peoples-people's people that I treasure because of my shameful mean Uncle Joe phase of life. (You do know famous folk don't just have assistant, their assistants have assistant assistants, who attend to your fan mail. Not sure some fans realize, you are a one way, one sided relationship-not a family member or friend. There's no avenue for most fans to directly contact ones such as Walsh, a huge celeb of fame, due to potential for danger, weirdos, nut-bags and recovering witches who could misinterpret communication.) So profound thanks to Joe's people's people!

18: *Compounded Substance*

Hiya N Honeys
Milestones N Monies
Jeans N Jokes
Rockn N Rowdy
Cowboys N Coke
Tunes N Totes
Duos N Dollars
Girls N Glory
Colorado N Cally
Suds N Studs
Denims N Dope
Babes N Blues
Indulgence N Indiscretion
Lures N Lust
Diabolical N Debauchery
Booze N Beats
Hits & Heat
Hoch & Hooters
Cash N Cars
Brash N Bars
Heaven N Hell
Restless N Ready
Cool N Collected
Spirited N Steady.

19: *A Family Band*

> The mama, the daddy
> the brothers of the band
> they ran around
> town to town
> playing their songs
> dancing their tunes
> tempting the law
> with a chainsaw
> Glenn was the man
> setting the rules
> Henley the drummer
> rocking since school
> the backup others
> brothers to brother
> doing their thang
> much like no other.

*Now, I always thought of the E band like a family: mom, dad, brothers, Uncle Joe, Cousin Satan...back in the earliest time it seemed Glenn was the daddy the ruling hand....The old married couple of parents dad and mom, certainly Henley and Glenn....looking back (forgive me one moment Papa Hen for looking back) but Glenn was their mama...because it's always the mother in the family that holds the final say...wears the pants...places the vote...and leads the others, makes major plans, and rules the land....(now, if your reading this message I hope you understand this is written only as ridiculousness and not in ill disrespect for these guys that of course I worship, families are unique crescendos but we love them dearly *and nobo*dy, absolutely nobody messes with our family).

20: *Vince Gill and the Eagles?*
November 10, 2017, Op-Ed

Vince Gill holds an incredible vocal song power. He has one astounding stunningly beautiful vocal voice. He is an exceptionally talented musician and songwriter and holds vast accomplishments in and as a country music veteran superstar.

Now, I have had to work really hard mentally to come to term with the fact that anyone would be on stage with the Eagles singing my beloved Glenn Frey's musical numbers. Vince covering a Glenn song? Can he? Could he perform and shine?

Through the years, there has been many cover band or individual singers who have sung Glenn or Eagles songs. Unlike the Eagles band, these are ones we can often afford concert price wise, and some are quite good at their dedication and craft. I see covers as a devotion to one great band. Henley states he does not.

In like manner, as an amateur novice on 'cover songs' I believed that when someone loved what you do so well as a band or with an admired song they wanted to use 'yours' that stands as an outstanding highly praised compliment for hey man fabulous job!

Some of our best singers use versions of cover songs. Henley, Eagles, Linda, Elvis, Clapton, Axl. Maybe, it doesn't count if you're already a smashing successful band. Don't most band start out covering others song? Pat Benatar had a huge success with a Mellencamp song. The Boss's first number one hit was performed by a cover band. They took Springsteen's song and "revved up like a deuce/shot loose like a deuce" running in the night.

None the else, cover songs or Eagles own version, if you were keen on Glenn you will probably not blink at welcoming Deacon Frey. He fits right into the mold to cover dad's music.

I realize it's really easy to like him. If you loved Glenn, you will be nuts over Deak. These Uncles are taking good care of him, guiding, training, teaching him more of what he and daddy started. They are preparing to gently nudge him forward for the edge of the nest. When he is ready, he will soar just like daddy. It's going to be an amazing take-off flight to witness.

As for the other newcomer, how has Vince come to fit into the remix? Some comment he is not up to E band's standard or say Gill is not a good fit. Others love his blended vocals with today's plan and band of merry wingmen.

Do this, do that, don't do this.... who are you; what gives you the right to determine who is the right ensemble? Well, I remember a time when I was inclined to feel Uncle Joe wasn't the right fit for the band. (Sorry, again I didn't *email* you Joe, but life is so good, and you are truly right, Glenn was great!) In reflection, what an imprudent perspective for Joe Walsh and yes, *I be one* ashamed gal of those past Walsh thoughts and words.

On the whole, some are begrudging while some are happy for this shuffle remix. Never gonna make everyone satisfied no matter what verdict is made by the valid decision-makers. I am sure they have been in the world long enough to know that fact.

Maybe as people state, Satan could possibly be some branch of VGill's management, as I would think he would have to be now to be touring with Eband.

Should I care, what do I know? No and absolutely nothing. Yet, if that is true then it explains so much about why he has ended up on touring and singing with the current band members. Are the 'Eagles' of today a cover band?

Will VGill now become and mold into a perfect configuration for this band? Is he needed? Does he bring in more revenue? More than Eagles alone could?

Personally, I'm not sure I buy into the fact that he was a close friend of Glenn's. Bowling, golfing, or simply being at a sporting event or fundraiser with someone does that make you a lifelong close personal companion? Do I know their connection, well no…?

And I never knew anything about Glenn other than what was out front on the stage floor or the minimal sharing he contributed on occasion. There are friends and acquaintances I know who were intertwined in some aspect of Glenn or Henley's world, but we don't discuss their personally connected relationships. Perfect example of my knowledge depth. I just longed to be a fan at a distant. Often fans may over emphasize, make perspective decisions and ideas on celebrities, and never truly know much of anything about them or their day to day world and personal acquaintances.

Prior to beginning his time with the E band, Gill contributed on Henley's music providing guitars and vocal harmony for recordings. In the late 80's at the Nashville City of Hope charity event there is a photo of Glenn with Eddie Rabbit and Vince Gill. Glenn said that during that week he met a lot of country music friends and that he was "only about two steps left of country music, anyway". Also, Vince introduced the band at '07 CMA's (they played "How Long"). So, ...so...

Maybe, it's just some unseen magnetic force that keeps taking care of the band.

Through the years, with ongoing transitions, the Eagles have continued to remain a powerfully strong, solid musical force. Fans remains unfaltering and have stayed faithful throughout all their decades of mayhem, triumphs, separations, victories, misfortunes, fortunes, and peace.

Moreover, their concerts continue to stay strong. And we still follow. The deejays continue to play their songs on the radio. And we still follow along. Records, CD's, tee shirts, merchandize sells rise upward. And we still continue to buy it all in masses. Their music continues to ignite us. And we still follow.

Even so, from day one of his begin, there was always something about Vince Gill that struck me inside. To better clarify, I don't mean joining this band, I mean from years ago. There was always admiration and joy from his music.

That Oklahoma born southern boy took to music like a cow to a salt lick. Musicians stated their perspective of Vince is he's a wonderfully humble, very nice grateful guy.

He has definitely proved himself, moves us with his music, and did very well in country music row. So, was this feeling a premonition of things to come following Glenn's absence or the lack of Bernie? Of course not.

In another step now, could my ideas on Eagles be that like so many others, I still have not come to term with the Bernie void? Was he invited back for the 2018 tour? What's interesting are comments supplied that Bernie likes to play country and bluegrass so we gonna swap him for the less country bluegrass dude V Gill? Less...really?

Maybe he doesn't wanta tour-well just say that; Henley has said BL doesn't like fame, just say that, whatever. It seems, if another guitar is needed to the stage floor **why is it not** Bernie Mathew Leadon III; he is the obvious choice.

This resurfaces frequently. I think fans just need and deserve some feedback answer addressed direct from Don Henley on why Bern is missing in action.

Now, it's quite easy to stand on the outside and pass judgement. I appreciate the fact that the decisions and the choices could be far worse for fans. There are musicians we wouldn't wanta see on stage with Eagles band.

In fact, I have a cousin that was deeply embedded in the music biz for a long time. She adamantly stated to me that of all the musicians she met or worked with, over the years, one of her favorites was VGill. She encouraged me to chill out and give Gill at shot at playing with the E's as he was wonderful, humble, and a very nice, sweet person; and she thought he would be meaningfully suited for the band.

I have always loved Vince Gill's song and video *"When I called your Name"* with Patty Loveless and their inspiration and raw emotion for *"Go Rest High on that Mountain"*. As well, his powerful striking songs like *"I Still Believe in You"*, *"Tryin' to get over You"*, *"I Never knew Lonely."* Such amazing vocal harmonies and focus in those songs. Just simply incredible talent and skill for writing and melodies.

I think most of all my issues are I want **my Glenn** to be there signing and yacking and tuning and playing. But he can't be. I miss Glenn and didn't ever realize that one day he would permanently not be on a stage with my band. For goodness sakes, I'm a nurse I know time eventually ends.·

Why didn't I realize? Glenn's and the others have done their own things on many diverse stages and all still succeeded well. But they returned to the E music and what a great day yesterday was. So sadly, now I will always be that *girl from yesterday*.

To biased me, Glenn was a star unique, different, engaging presence that held one incredible spellbinding fine-tuned persona on stage. Would the lack of that personality be noticed? Would it be Eagles that returned or a cover version?

In some weird means, I seemed to be giving Gill a lot of grief and making him suffer for something that is not even of his own violation. I think over time, my resentment of Vince will hopefully soften, and I can come to accept these things as another part of our band's shift.

Honestly, I am trying to cut Vince Gill a smidgen of slack. I do want him to fit especially because Henley is all in with him being in the band. And I am a devoted follower of the rule: Don Henley is always right. I do revere Vince's voice and talents. Vince thoughtfully stated he "knew it was my voice that had something special about it" (for his ears told him!)

Further, most would not be able to watch Gill and Patty Loveless sing "Go Rest HOTM" at GJones Memorial service and not be moved by his compassion and emotion during this tribute. It was an extremely touching, powerful and a wholehearted-felt displayed moment of many country music souls, under that one roof, adjoined by Loveless and VGill.

Moreover, I am happy for Vince that he gets to have fun on stage with our band. I am confident it is a dream of a lifetime for him to play music with the Eagles band.

Of course, this is a huge bonus to him and his wife's career and will polish any vague faded reminders of their remarkable past musical appeal as the newer generation evolves. There is no downside in any fashion that I can see for Gill or his talented wife with his joining the E touring band team.

Either way they are both exceptionally skilled artisans. Further, I don't mean with the band, but I expect her or Vince to be on some stage or recording studio, each performing duets, with Henley anytime soon; it is coming, you can feel it floating in the air.

For the most part, Vince is an Eagle associate now; he is more than likely here to stay.

21: *A Hot Band of Thawed-out Brothers (HFOT)*

Hallelujah, finally the band has reunited and is back on the road again. Maybe, better friends and music men than ever before. Rolling along like it's 70's once more.

Glenn Frey once pronounced Eagles band of the Seventies was the phase where we "got crazy, got drunk, got high, had girls, played music and made money… (and had the greatest parties of the seventies)."

One reason that they endured and have returned to unify for "Hell Freezes Over Tour" (HFOT) *could be* that they compose honest, distinctive bold songs and enjoyed that group partnership. Thank goodness that 'forgiveness' kicked in.

Seriously, they each hold focus, rhythm, style and reveal labored layers of meaning, the songs, **and** the singers. Each singer in this band is multi-talented and well-versed in his own right. As for the songs, while these songs are decades old, they continue to remain current and seem fresh, true, and modern.

They bond us. They bonded them. Their songs never departed from our radio airwaves playlist, our lips, our heads, or our hearts. And their songs are our shared storied lives and link to the same meaning for our own occurrences; our own song playing out in their wordings.

It's a great relief to fans that the Eagles are ready to return.

Glenn and Henley commented basically they were living their own lives doing their own thing and did not see each other like they wanted to because of responsibilities. Maturity, responsibility, and separation periods can produce major change, awakening, acceptance, and appreciation to our lives.

Also, I think Travis Tritt-that one known as the 'maverick' of the country music class of '89 newcomers (or the hatless, leatherwearN, long-haired, honkytonk hippy rebel, oh yeah!) could be more responsible for this Eagles returning reunion than we may know…maybe not. Or maybe, I just want him to be appreciated because he's a good old Southern boy and excellent musician. So, if he is in any fashion a minor uniting link, bless that amazing Marietta Georgia born country music, unique, bewildering outlaw.

As for the band, there is no refuting things are the same but that 'they' are different. They are working through more transitions, unsure of what or probably where this new enterprise leads. If they build it, the fans will come, the loyal E fans will always come. I do not know that they realize, from my opinion, what a massive fanbase they command, braves who would follow them into battle, fight through the fire and back, still standing by our warriors of flight.

Still, I think on a most intimate team sport kinda level Glenn, Henley, Tim, Uncle Jo, Satan, even Bernie and Randy value and accept each other despite any differences. Randy noted after leaving "I don't want hate in my life…it's hard on the heart…will make you old and bitter".

No wonder so many often refer to him as 'sweet Randy'.

Now, while some members have ventured more into other areas of life and play, they understand each other in ways many others never will. I think they, as well as Azoff, like the world to be mystified by their band and music.

Some men see things as they are and ask "why?
But I dream things that never were" and ask why not?
-(George Bernard Shaw-BUT I betta this is probably Irving Azoff's Motto!?!)

I feel they learned to appreciate the gifts and purpose each one held for the other. For them and us we are all healing together. Growing and rocking onward. Despite the struggles of life, we find our bearings and our blessings.

During his solo days Glenn dedicated *"Desperado"* to his songwriting companion and sang the song just as perfectly pitch and smooth as Henley. Despite this being during the eighty's years and time of their pausing exodus Glenn as well stated, one of his potential goals was to "make a record as good as Don Henley's". Maybe you see those words in other light, but I see it as admiration for his distinct friend and partner.

As fans, we live in another parallel universe from theirs. We hold our ideas and perspectives on their world, but we probably know so little…Spilt, separations, solos, divorce, hiatus they still have degrees of respect for each other, like bloodlines.

Overall, they share their stories with and for us in real time through each song. The rides, the journeys, the realities, the loves, the losses, the isolations, and even the messiness we all have to handle in our own situations and in our ways as well.

Yet maybe they don't share all their stories. That's probably a really good thing. Maybe one reason as well for so few interviews with the band was, they like their privacy and plausible suspense. Henley always stated they hold many things close to their chest. Well, I know that I have essentially figured one of those things out. An Eagle Secret Revealed: *'teniamo fra noi'* (Shhhh, this is just between us fans).

Don Henley selected the wrong state to imply where he was raised. **Do**

you think Henley is from the south? Texas, please. Listen to the man speak. Glenn was a whole lots more southern country than Hen ever could be…Glenn was always ain't, can't, wanna, gonna, gravy…are those Detroit street words?

But we have to believe Henley if he implies, he is from Texas. He says his mother was a schoolteacher. Ever heard a child of a schoolteacher speak with a poor tongue (and he does say the word 'yawl' in *"LIT Fast Lane"*) …hmm… ok HenHen…ok. So, I guess I better give him some valuable credit for being a sophisticated southern. We Southerners are mighty proud of him and honored that he is from the great state of Texas. As is said: "Well, God bless Texas!"

Easy for me to understand, which is the southern desperado. (Maybe I just want Glenn too to be southern…you think?) …

Another matter, I didn't really appreciate when the band went into a nosedive split. *What do you mean the Eagles broke up!?!* That's high school Friday night boyfriend words for the weekend. Broke up? We gotta have that music to survive and find our way into our twenties, life, relationships, choices. How are fans supposed to find their way without our band?

Thank goodness for radio loyalist deejays, special performances, tours, and their solo career staying power as singers and songwriters. I think now that the HFOT has begun in full swing it has made me realize that the dating relationship breakup was overall good for each of them.

They went out and showed the world that they could make their way in whatever fashion means they desired. They established themselves individually. They didn't have to return after fourteen years, they had made it…proved what they needed, earned all they needed, became grounded, began to have impressive personal family lives as well, outstanding achievements and accomplishments, and came a long, long way in life.

So, why would they return to the band?

They are a family unit. They make the music the world needs and diehard fans love and enjoy. It's obvious they love it too. That's the sign of a full-fledged musician. They never stop…the music keeps playing.

Our hope is rooted into their return, into their new outcomes. And as fans, we are so grateful they are back, going strong as ever!

22: *Touring from the road*

Ashes to ashes, dust to dust
you may play with big boys
but you can hang with us?

Border to border, hand to hand
roaming around
we take our stand.

Town to town, city to city
setting the stage
those steel roadies pave the way.

Corner to corner, land to land
you may handle big boys
but only Eagles play in this band.

23: *Eagles Posterity*
October 21, 2009, Op-Ed

I desired for so long for there to be an Eagles Museum. I can't image how many 'mementos' they hopefully have stored safety in secure multi-warehouses somewhere. Hopefully, well preserve for posterity.

Once, while in Texas, I asked one of Henley's friend's if any of their solo or band's memorabilia was in the Smithsonian. I wanted the answer to be of course girlie you just missed it on all those trips to DC.

I had all the accoutrement in my head they needed to donate, so I just shared with him, so he could be sure that Don Henley listened to my wisdom and guidance (ha!). Bernie Leadon's banjo, Timmy's fringed Native American suit, Randy's black silk (Japanese) "Eagles" jacket, Don Henley first Slingerland three piece red-sparkle drum kit his mama brought him from McKay's Music Co in Sulphur Springs (yeah like he'd give that away-I wouldn't either), Satan's middle finger (yikes ok maybe just that picture of him on the desk giving the what for), Walsh's red brick pantsuit and that red bandana, and Frey's classic 'Number-One' Takamine 6-strings acoustic-electric guitar, that black 'University of Colorado' tee, a black wrist sweatband, and his aviator shades (it would have been nice to have a lock or two of that Glenn hair but so be it...).

I am confident Henley got the word and is working on this just for me...I am going to be patient because I have heard him rattle off his list plans for the future and Jesus it's mighty loooooooong.

I also asked why no star on the Hollywood walk of fame but was told (unsure so don't quote me) that they didn't want to appear and that they said no thanks. Well, ok. I know they told many no thanks, but I sure would like for them to have one for the band and one each for their solo music which is just as important and valuable to fans as their works together as a band.

Would I be selfish to ask for so many squares for our greatest American band?

Of course, as had been shared and videotaped at least **all** seven members of the band were on stage for the Rock 'n' Roll Hall of Fame induction ceremony of 1998 (or the indictment!) and joyfully sang together as one unified family band.

I always thought musicians were as F Scott Fitzgerald wrote of that you hold two thoughts in your mind simultaneously with the ability to use your intelligence to function cognitively at the same time. The E's must have held that magical ability to function while doing two things at one time, playing, singing, entertaining, reading the setlist, oops-well that more than two, guess that makes them first-rate high-class intelligent geniuses…

Myself, being unable to perform two tasks at one time, I can't *chew and walk gum* (no not typo-just an 'Anita thang'). But if I could, I would be doing just that in LA at the Walk of Fame looking downward seeking their star recognition slabs.

I can continue to hope for future concrete blocks and rewarded acknowledgement, right? With any luck, my gait and eyesight will last long enough to one day walk, chew walked gum, look down, and find their imprints right there on a sacred sidewalk…well, a silly, low-skilled, introverted girl can dream…

24: *Jamm'N 4 Timmy*
December 15, 2016, Op-Ed

In all the years that I have written about the Eagles there really has been almost no mention of Timothy. He appears to be calm, quiet, overall well-mannered and respectful. But I really don't know much about Mr. S so regrettable maybe that's why I have avoided penning about him.

Timothy, who for me is essentially 'Timmy' even though I have heard him say he really didn't appreciate being called Timmy. Still, I impolitely do it ongoing. Extremely difficult for me to break any habit. Please forgive me son.

Well, already off track on notation for Tim. So, since I am on the me topic, for me Timmy character comes across as the sweet, adorable, low-key silent one. Like Randy, both are quiet reserved bass player that kinda vanishes sometimes on the stage scene.

Even when Timothy sings 'his' songs there are times you forget that it's his turn to shine for suddenly there's Joe, Glenn, Henley doing their thang which could easily distract from the considerate timid Schmit.

Each member possesses a deep rich distinct genuine vocal uniqueness that meshes and flows completely into and around the others. Possibly why the band's harmonies were so profound.

Like Randy Meisner style as well Timmy holds a beautiful mellow voice. Soft, collected, pleasant unhurried gentle pitch, soothing high hitters for the rafter's singers.

My favorite Timmy song has always been Poco's *"Keep on Trying"*. Timmy wrote the song and sang lead on this tune, which happens to be Poco's biggest hit record of 1975.

Don't get me wrong, I love hearing TBS sing vocals with our band or solos numbers. '*I can't tell you why*' but his tunes are all soft, airy, with the perfect tempo, tone, melody. His voice bridges so well with all the other guys. I know like me, people appreciate and admire him and his talent, yet he is definitely the wallflower, often fading into the background on our bands stage. Guess on stage with Uncle Joe, Glenn, and Henley someone had to be the calm silent majority.

A minor personal tidbit, TBS wife an actress Jean Cromie-Schmit was

Ethereal Woman in the movie "This is Spinal Tap". They have been married since 1984.

Sadly, I yelled at Timmy once.

Can you image anyone yelling at kind, humble, introverted TBS. Well, it was in fact at the TV. But, but, but, yet, yet, yet, still it's was in response for Timmy's wording. He stated during the hiatus or 14-year vacation that he hustled by working with Jimmy Buffett, Toto, Twisted Sister, Warren Zevon, Dan Fogelberg, Poison & others. Amazing! I love these bands excellent choices.

But he commented that he wouldn't get credit and it was mostly yelling. So, I added my own yelling. Firmly, but like him with no half Detroit words.

Wow, now Timmy son, this is an impressive list of assets to your musical resume. There were of course many vast acquirable talents they could have used but they saw your ability and were eager to work with you. That was truly an honor to be asked to collaborate with these exceptional musicians.

How diverse your talent must be, how compelling and blessed you were to be a part of these acts. You were doing what you loved, taking care of your family, and making it in the music world. You did well, you survived.

It may have gotten rough sometimes but in the long run you did so good. We are truly proud of and for you. Rework that wording into more positive thought process for future communicates about this period son-Hey, *'we're not gonna take'* negative reflective spin (ha).

Seconds after my unnecessary tirade he did go on to share much from my own rant. If, I would have just calmed down and given him the minute he deserved...

In reality, Timothy Bruce as well had impressive performance, toured or played with the likes of Bob Seger, Richard Marx, Sheena Easton, Steely Dan, Clint Black, Vince Gill, Firefall, Ringo Star, Crosby, Still, Nash and many more.

And it would be just plain wrong not to mention his collaboration on Seger's *'Fire Lake"* or Boz Scaggs *"Look What You Done to Me"*. Gossip has queried that maybe he was a tap-dancing youngster, perhaps where his stylish moves come into play...Undoubtfully, we have seen that Timothy is a great juggler. Last and maybe kinda vital to music fans it was our Timmy who coined the famous term **'Parrothead'**, I am sure Jimmy B is beaming!

His latest solo album *'Leap of Faith'* was released in September 2016 is his sixth studio album and he dedicated this to Glenn as: *"To Roach From Woodstock"*. He states, 'this is who I am' and it's all written by Timmy himself. I am confident Glenn; I mean Roach would be so proud of and for Woodstock.

Timothy also provides that he recorded the songs for this album at his home studio in the Santa Monica Mountains of his home state California. LOF has some wonderful style and song elements to it and I am sure Timmy will make more solo records in the future.

So basically, I am truly blessed to have seen him perform on stage with others but never during solo shows. Maybe that would be a solid New Year Resolute; an achievable but I don't make 'em as I don't believe in Resolutions. If you wanta make a change you will. New Year, old year, or mid-year.

All the same, hope to see you flying and singing onward Mr. Timothy for a long, long time, somewhere down your peaceful easy red dirt road. Hang in son, we're all taking this *leap of faith* with you. Or as Glenn would say 'with ya'.

25: *Fragile Uncertainty*

Life is only momentary. Then, when disaster, grief, death, change, catastrophe is happening to you personally it seems to be the end of the world. Life instantly freezes-a crashing stop. An internal destruction is inevitable. Misery, desolation, a tornado. An ocean of storm charged emotions impact. A cyclone meeting a hurricane, which promises head-on waves colliding. Tossing adrift in tumbling waters, sinking because you are unable to move enough to paddle.

Night, day, actions move on automatic routine. Darkness exposes like a halogen light shutdown of power, knocked out during an electrical storm. A sudden overwhelming total obscured blackness. A candle snuffed out by wind. No glowing ember after a log fire goes to cold ash. No light, no radiance, no glimmer of hope.

Glenn sang *"You are not alone, you're not..."* That statement on its own should bring us 'hope'.

For me, Glenn's music transformed me, his spirit motivated me, his hair thrilled me, his talent riveted me, his drive inspired me, his mystique awestruck me, his determination moved me, his smile drugged me, his passing crushed me. Surrounded by numbness, you hold on to a myriad of emotions that just don't make sense.

How do you cope with the sudden fallout? How do you wake from this mentally induced coma? How do you turn the page? How do you ever get up out of the total inky descending bottomless well of pain? Probably most critical, how do you heal?

Life around you and the rest of the world rapidly move forward, perpetual motion. Click, click, click, back to the pitch, while you live stuck in a ditch. Something is wrong with this concept. One of the biggest process from loss, change, heartbreak is to never take one single second, one day, one band of brothers, one individual you have been blessed to know for granted.

After an eleven years run on CBS 'The Carol Burnett Show' came to an end. In only his finest witty way Tim Conway wanted to express to Carol what she meant to him. Of course, it's Toma Conway (no misprint) so he didn't just send her a sweet little ole card and nice vase of flowers; oh no way, he wrote her a special goodbye skit that was published in "Variety". "THE GOOD-BYE SKETCH" (Carol and Tim): ... (Tim Conway/Variety 1978).

If you read his notation you will understand that his words of "time" and "his thanks" paragraph-that meant so much to him (and to me). I really related my feelings and emotions on Glenn's passing after rereading Conway's words yet once more. They were exactly what I wanted to state to Glenn Frey about how his music influenced and helped all his fans along life's pathway if I would have had the chance.

NOTE-If you are an ardent Eagles band fan you understand exactly where Tim Conway was coming from; how someone special can be so refreshingly entertaining that they hold the natural ability to beneficially change your mood, your lifespan, your dance step, your spirit, your day.

SECTION SIX: MUSIC

*"Music expresses that which cannot be
put into words and that which cannot remain silent."*
~ (Victor Hugo)

 # 1: *The singing heart...*

Your heart still sings
as black birds gather
your heart still sings
it's light as a feather
your heart still sings
pure as lace and leather
your heart still sings
in strings of measure
your heart still sings
that voice brought treasure
your heart still sings
some chords sounded better
your heart still sings
casts blue styled tunes
your heart still sings
our friends come together
your heart still sings
but I truly rather
your heart just beat
in your pumping chest
than feel it stop
and be at rest.

2: *That power of the music*

The power of music moves over the soul
brilliant colorful strings of pastels so bold
passionate hearts rock any dream whole
creative melody's rhythm soaked in pure gold.

Mesmerizing thoughts, meshing of words
adrenaline rush excitement, for all one's worth
beats live as tunes roll, harmony for the soul
powerful tempting vessel, crossing shear goal.

Painting artwork with each stroke of word
the tapestry colored music echoes that surge
the canvass recognition distinct releasing purge
different lyrics expression dipped in ink emerge.

3: *THE STORY OF MUSIC*

Music is a story.
Listen.

Music is deeply rooted in our core.
It's our safe place.
Just listen.
Close your eyes.
Feel it.
Listen.
Let it move through our soul.
It's a story.
It's a refugee, a joy, a theme.
If gives us a place to
run away from-to escape.
It transports.
It's part of our culture.
It's a simple design.
It can imitate our feelings,
our needs, our motions,
cries, laughter, our silence.
It's an avenue to let go.
Listen.

The voice, the instrument, the composition,
the personality, the conduit.
It's about an awareness, a movement,
an uplifting spirit, love,
lack of love, a richness, openness,
freshness, a shelter.
Just listen.

Music gives hope, creation,
voice, force, concert, space.
Uplifting or heartbreaking,
soothing or ecstatic.

Listen.
Listen, it's a story.

4: *Flatlined*

Symphonies rose to life, hearts soar
their beat climatically pumping
rapidly swaying playful jumps
how can a broken heart pump
why doesn't it stop suddenly at once?

5: *The Musical Compass*

Music is our compass
can drives the soul to sin
directing the roadmap
lectures from within
roaming down the highway
playing toward the east
or pushing past the west
guiding us along
through the journey home
singing us a quite song
or belting a pop fellow
EltonJ or JLo tell her
that's there's cool rays
in the rainbow's yellow
or around the next bend
teaches where to send
rolling down the path
without directional guide
staying on the course
exit ramps or unseen detours
sometimes they arise
to create a dire scene of chaos

right before our very eyes.

6: *Soundless Expression*

Just below the surface
many thoughts swirl around

word or phrase lay internal churning
no verbal sound is screamed or made

no voice is heard aloud mute tone
hangs inside, on silent cloud they stay

quite imagination builds
bold, forceful, clear and loud

declaration has to wait within
where no other resonance bounce

reflection of these particles
collectively arranged leap crashing abound

reverberation sits in the inter-working
of a mind, notions flutter falls all around

echoes in the jungle shout so loud
but no accent call comes out of the sound.

7: *The tone of the Music*

Music:
the sound, the words, the soul,
the beat, the singer, the song
touch us in a means that is
unparalleled, unmatched to other
methods of contact communication.
An awakening reminder that music.
It's a powerful force a vibration
of meaning that can give peace, comfort,
mementos of now, them, then,
or serve as a source of emotional healing.
It can hit you on the head, smack you
flat in the face, punch you out of the chair
get you on the dance floor, lift the spirit to soar.
That voice, that tune, that beat,
that movement, of course that chorus.
It rocks us forward, holds us in space,
taps our shoulder of pass time,
pass feeling, pass living, pass dealing.

8: *Music Is A Celebration*

Music is a composed release
holds healing power
stands as a coping method
during happy, content, or bad woes.

Music is an emotional means
a transformational tower
it's a safe travel experience
during desolate, joyous, or sad dark hour.

Music is a power tool
it grinds, sands, or drills
industrial instrument that
sets our electrical circuit to rule.

Music is a flowing stream
to move one forward
it's assembly of hope
giving way for a surface to float.

Music is like planting a seed
and watching it grow
it produces a show
that sings, goes, and flows.

Music is a dream
full of potential means
to arrive with a forceful
thrive to be alive.

Music is remembrance
of excitement, grief, or sharing
giving survivors journey a caring labor
of control that comforts the soul.

9: *Sing a tune find some spice for life it's going to be alright*

Like a rocket to the moon
you took off from our lives too soon
you had to leave you had to go
but we are sad we are slow.

In getting pass this dreadful mass
which took from us a special lad
with your style and with your
brazen grace you held a sacred class.

But we were just truly blessed
that you even came along
and gave to us happy songs
yet you left and took our jingle.

So, when we think of you today
we sing the tunes you gave us many
and they were very fine the kind you
drink slow with chilled red wine.

And in the times we lose our way
we will think of the days
you enriched and served us well
gave us joy and rang the bell.

Or on a night when things aren't steady
and we forgot the key to the Chevy
or on a day in late May when things
are gray and we need our say.

To deal with this dismantled steal
that you now live there in a new land
in a different home and we are left
back here to ourselves, cold and alone.

10: *The music's breathing therapy*

Crescendo of vital music makes us close our eyes.
We stop and just breath as all our energy sources
focus on only our breath-listening, feeling the music.

That connection to the beauty of each beat as it pulses
through our veins produces a soothing serenity-
masterpiece of therapy that melts stone, heals pain.

11: *Give Me a Music Man*

A dedicated musician
can take the word
create a heap
that when purged
urged and surged
leaps up from
the page
the voice, the fingertips
that spark accord and
sing with joy or occur
a beat when struck
with pitch displays
a cord, a note
a tune of time
a quick street feat
steaming with heat
that shocks spring
to bare raw feet.
A dedicated musician
can make one feel
he's seen your heart
walked in your step
reviewed your soul
dreamed that dream
lived that adventure
captured your minute
but most of all
composed a verse
shared some moment
in time, space or place
with only you
and you alone
know what streamed
through your own
street, journey, road
or your own song.

12: *The music following*

Rock n' roll
is organized religion
faith, prayer, worship
sainted words that churn
tunes lacking slow burn
volumes for maxi loud
turn it up beats played proud
gut-wrenching sound
awe wowing crowd.
Rock 'n' roll
it's a craft
fuels the soul
hall of famers
it's nostalgia
is that the answer
for those destiny players
playing on fearlessly designed
masterfully created and stated.

13: *The Music of Voices*

When you open your mouth do you listen what comes out.
When you speak, do you hear, what others hear.
What tosses forth, what is the course of your voice, is it low.
Do you have a Scottish rouge, do you speak foreign or slow.
Have you gained the great white plains, Boston thrill it sure is real.
When you bless their hearts oh so much do they know your Southern touch.
Pitch it high as Finnish can, do you answer pale, chilled and kind.
The Irish speak 'O-so fine, rolls off the tongue like a fine wine.
The Philly Steak tone, Minnesota twain jargon is flat cold as winter snow.
The five boroughs tenors they do roam, call New Y their frickN' home.
The tangy drawl of a good Tex is a star standing lingo strong.
The English style makes us smile, chats with Aussie mates, go a mile a minute.
The peaceful, easy, mellow throat-ed feeling of Cally sun, surf,
desert dream has good pitch.
The tone, the slang the language notes where you're from, be it lively or absurd.
Do you judge any man, by the way in the air on which they hang their words there?

14: *SOILD GOLDEN APPRECIATION*

Golden days of yester remind us that we were loyal rock 'n roll baby boomers. Ladies and Gents of those seventies and eighties living on the edge for the heart of rock n roll.

Now, aging Rock Star super legends are speeding rapidly passing fifty. Those who gave us awesome music, lived hard, partied hard, full of rough tough living. Took the phrase sex, drugs, and RnR to heart. Ones such as KISS, Gun N Roses, Lynyrd Skynyrd, Journey, Aerosmith, Cher, Survivor, Melissa Etheridge, Billy Joel, Phil Collins, Joan Jett, Foreigner, Stones, Jon Bon Jovi, Heart, Bob Seger and of course Eagles and many others. *

Age affects us all. Now, some are becoming struggling tourers, who are living on a scared prayer or borrowed time. Our groupie fan club members are getting older as well. Rock Stars start young and are supposed to burn out at thirty. Isn't that the expectation? Discipline, hard physical work, dedication, determination gets tougher with aging. Touring must be so rough.

If music follows past patterns the idea is to push out the old ones. Yet while not all, most newer music choices are basically objectionable. The oldies are just plain better.

When history looks back it has 'clear-eyes'. Retrospection. Today, is current music engaging, mystifying, cool, relatable, unique, understandable?

Last live Eagles concert, I looked around to realize, not all, but many souls under that roof were mature aging adults. Rocking hip music loving folks that appeared over forty. 'Twisted' with the arthritis, 'popping' NSAID's, smelling of Ben-Gay instead of 'smelling' of hootie-weed. Smoke at times hung in the air but it was produced from a machine.

Some might have been stones and blurry eyed but was it kidney stones and cataracts? Some might have been stumbling and tripping BUT it was a different kind of 'trip'.

When we were growing into adolescence, we were picky. Yet, we had good choices. In our state of mind our music was not an entire industry of wreckage. We understood music 'took our stand', 'played our hand' and we used it's means to seek escape and identity in songs.

Golden days youth, adolescence, fun days, sun days, filled our inquiring aging minds.

Today, our greatest generation of music plays on, for a good ole classic *never* goes out of style just plays on and on for a slow country mile. These outstanding aging bands still rock our world, today going strong. How do they keep up? How do they stay fit? How can they stay on tune and on their toes without missing a beat? Rock music is not for the weak of heart.

Golden Days. Aging it's not for the weak of heart.

When you look in the mirror suddenly one day you ponder who is that looking back at me? Reflective reflection. Golden Aging?

So, I gotta go. I got a lot living left to do. Golden Living.

---

* Out of respect, I feel I have the need and responsibility to refer that Glenn and Henley demanded they were not Rock Stars. Still, to me they were Super Sensational Rock Stars.

15: *Blessed*

To the end of the world and back
fate tied us together no hack
destiny's chance tossed its stack
there was pure joy that's a fact.

A fortune was won
with the voice of a song
a tune for all times
all setlists were long.

A casual coincidence
well not a chance
we all came along
for a song and a dance.

A quirk some fluke
or was it all luck
that brought the E band
to LA to all of us.

The chance they took
was a toss of the jacks
it was just pure joy
what a dynamic fact.

16: *Manipulations Turn*

A force of nature
can sting or burn
can bring about a
play that churns
spins about another tale
one of bright days
sunshine or hale
nature's forces
come and go
come to life
and won't let go
up or down
it will bring
it's beat
for a while
awake or sleep
it comes to town
to run aground
it moves along
it sings its song
some songs are fine
some songs are blue
it rises up whenever
it must it last
for hours or for a day
it comes along
whenever it may.

17: *SLAYER PLAYER MAN*

He plays white lightin' on fortified guitar strings
oh my gosh he makes those steel strings sings
his face distorted, his tongue he may chew
but the songs he sings
we eat 'em up like a fine stew.
Once upon a time he liked booze and the women
he still into Fenders but needs no more benders
for now he's sober and content with good ole living
without the need of wine, brew, rough drillin'
his soul is content mild, sunny, and chillin'.
He prances & dances all over the stage
he makes us smile, he makes our day
the music he plays at any show are now less die-set
but when he plays, we adore all his frets
who knew an Eagles could make such a great blasted clearheaded pet!
Joe truly gets the crowds a-rockin', we come from a far, we are a-flockin'
when Joe pounds that stage, we all are engaged
like a wild animal pried loose from his deep cage
his songs set the tone, his riffs raise the blaze
for he's now a different sounding man with a sane take and gaze.

18: *Sequenced Composition*

Roses are red violets are blue
I can pen a poem and you can too
Roses are red the sky's up high
if the words rhyme is it a pie
Roses are red how do you crone
a verse of music a song for June
Roses are red it takes some luck
to spin to soar to float like a duck
Roses are red said the dish and the spoon
turn the page read tall tales of the cocoon
Roses are red out on the sand dunes
when loons shout out loud sounds boom
Roses are red and when it's all done
it will sing back it's tune like the silvery moon.

"That music in itself, whose sounds are songs, the poetry of speech." (Lord Byron)

SECTION SEVEN: BRIEF MENTIONS
ON EAGLES, MUSICIANS, EAGLES FRIENDS, ASSOCIATES IN OTHER TOPIC ARTICLES
(& SOME PERSONAL OPINION MATERIALS)

"...my heart with raptured thrills...let music swell the breeze, and ring from all the trees...let mortal tongues awake; let all that breathe partake... the sound prolong,,,to thee we sing...."
~ ("America", Rev Samuel F Smith), (1832)

#1: *That running dream*
July 2, 2010, Special Feature

I am a confirmed runner! I began running by running. It's kinda changed my life.

Sometimes well-mannered people run. Jackson Browne, Bruce Jenner, Ted Bundy, Juice Simpson (no now not that run-the running back racing through the airport and before buying white Broncos running), John Edwards, Forrest Gump. Go Forrest, run Forrest run, run.

Running has become a huge part of my life. It's almost become an obsession. An addiction that in some ways I like a little too much. Running to the point of windy breaths. You know the point. Running, running, running. Well, mentally running.

Of course, I defiantly don't mean the type where you put on your gym shorts, tie your shoelaces, grab a water bottle and the stopwatch cause I'm gonna pound the pavement till I sweat rubber runner type. Oh no, not that at all. That thought makes me pour sweat, feel nauseous and start to cry.

In other words, I only mean the simple-minded non-hyperventilating running type. And real running ain't like no good ole box of chocolate!

Specifically, I just seem to be constantly on the run. I am always running usually because of tardiness. At least now I can blame it on age. I am late running for appointments, running late for deadlines, running late to return calls, late running for dinner (well not that one as often).

Sadly, I just seem to have fallen into this bad habit of being a non-punctual runner. I never appreciated it when others were running late. I didn't understand their lack of non-existent time frames or day planners. How rude, I would always mentally comment.

Well, now I seem to be a runner. One of 'those.' Running. Ah, running. Running to the car, running toward the washing machine, running through the house, running with the beat of the music, running after the mailman (oops I mean mail person-gotta get it politically correct).

Forrest Gump was a great runner. Look how much ground that kid covered. In the wind, rain, burning desert sun, jumping, and running in cemented ponds, across corn fields and through miles and miles of asphalt covered locales. And look what all he accomplished while doing some of his little jogs. Roared clean clear over Bear Bryant's football field, met Presidents, raced through exploding fire balls, zoomed straight off shrimping boats. Even due to running, created smiley face. Then, suddenly the child had some epiphany.

What a stroke of luck-may have been the heat. He realized it was time to go home. He just quit running, put the past in the past, went running (well walking) back toward not against the breezy floating winds of Alabama, Savannah Georgia, a park bench, family, and destiny. 'Stop' running Forrest.

But what is so unfortunate, unhealthy, and distressing is I seem to be running through life. I want to sit down, breath, enjoy. However, I do seem to do a lot of sitting, but that sitting includes running...

Way back in the day, ole ole days before Hoover and F Gump, God must have invented running. Lot's wife was running, look where that got her. Jonah was on a running adventure, ran right into the belly of that whale. Daniel was running and he ended up in the Lion's den. Joseph ran and he ran in an elaborate expensive coat. He probably should have used that coat of many colors to bargain his way out of his dilemma. But, unfortunately, he came from a jealous family of thieving sinners; for instance, his brothers stole that multi-colored coat. Well, damaged or not, at least he had something to show off as the results of his running.

All the same, if they had all been only mentally running, wouldn't their lives have been so much simpler...Forrest Gump, perfect example. His running motor finally clicked on (or wore out) and he went home to be a more low-keyed mental runner, a quite fisherman, a modest lawn mower king, and a meek southern daddy-bless his humble pea picken' heart.

Thus, as per the brilliant one-liner of Forrest Gump enough said about that. Now, if I could just get the mental running muster to cognitively venture toward that dust covered treadmill, boy I am confident some mental pound would melt away somehow and I wouldn't have to be so concerned with the health matters...well so a girl can dream about running...Dream on...run Forrest run...run Anita run...run...

2: *Memory Provokers or the Camp 'Pledge'*
January 16, 2013, Op-Contributor

Pictures, music, video, smells, cards, books, voices, eyes. Few elements evoke emotions of memory. Happy times, younger times, family, troubled days, holidays, voids, journeys. Reminders of other places, times, people, events.

Childhood misadventures gone awry ensue when you happen to be born into a household of brothers. Oh, the tales we could share...one of the biggest nightmares, I mean blessings of my youth, was being born to a man that loved adventures. Not only adored them but yearned to learn together and share with his kids.

Whew, those adventure lessons. My dad greatest quality is grade-A, top-notch, deeply committed tolerance for patience. He could have made Job, Adam, Eve, Noah, and Moses sin.

Daddy never hurried, never rushed, and had to read every single noted letter of instruction and understand all before opening any box, item, package, tool, toy, etc. Then, every single thing has to be laid out in certain order. He didn't just measure twice...no wonder we are a gang of perfectionist children (or slight control freaks...).

Still, we learned about sports, board games, historical sites, Hot Wheel race tracks, ping pong, pets, Atari, cracking coconuts, toasting chestnuts (ever tried cracking toasted c-nut?) gardening, badminton, flying kites, masonry, science (yawn), math (double yawn/yawn nasty, nasty, nasty) fishing-oh lord help us all aka patience in waiting, long, long waiting & much more awfully nasty than math.

But probably my biggest nightmare adventure was around eight or nine-ish years when daddy decided he would teach lessons on camping, fire, tents, and the stars. Camping, camping, camping-Jesus Christ holy mother of the sainted virgin, I wish I knew some of Glenn Frey's Detroit half-words...camping.

When you are a spoiled rotten southern princess, roughing it is not found in your Webster, your vocal, your patience or your understanding. Roughing it is when you are forced to go to the Overnight Inn Roadside Express because the Four Seasons doesn't have a room!

Lying in a cloth sleeping bag on the ground in a tent with a thin cloth flooring between your bag and the dirt-not my cup of tea. Wooden stakes, poles, firewood, flint, outdoor bathrooms-I was a girl for goodness sake. Does this sound like things a princess would enjoy?

Gathering rocks, finding wood, trying to start a fire waiting for stakes to be driven into the ground. Waiting for the fire to get hot enough, then waiting for the hot-dogs to be slightly warm dogs...waiting, waiting.

Moreover, I forbade myself from discussing the fear of South Georgia bugs (bugs, spiders, skeeters, snake-take your pick, you can have 'em-no wonder I love the indoor activities...). But the greatest sum of all my most dire fears, camping...

By early nightfall, the fire embers dimly glowing, tent sorta aligned, sleeping bags unfurled, burnt marshmallows consumed, The Milky Way quizzes and explanations, the ghoulish ghost stories started I had had enough.

Taking my shaky flashlight and after much stressful complaining, complaining, complaints, I fumbled the roughly thirty-two yards or so into the house from the backyard, aka tent land, praying the batteries would last until I made it inside to my bed (aka Goddess Heaven.) Aww. Believe me nobody had to remind me that night to say my goodnight prayer to John-Boy Walton.

So, while yes, I was tough enough to survive that horror tale, which created a prolong eternal fear of camping, I did learn an extremely valuable lesson in oaths. That night Me and Scarlet solemnly took 'The Pledge' with God as our witness never to never, ever, ever 'ruff it again'.

For as long as I can find a bed, sofa, or recliner to fall into...I hereby solemnly swear that I shall promise to uphold the sanctity of that honorable pledge forever until death. That night, I proudly verbally signed the pledge, took that oath, and stand firm to date.

Now I realize there are many that love camping. God bless your soul; I am happy for each of you. On the ground is not somewhere I enjoyed lying down upon. A thin strip of cloth or bagged, no thanks. Star gazing, I can appreciate and do today on the internet-two-legged star type or twinkling star from the telescope (bless modern technology).

Many, many ventures, many moons and rough days later I am grateful and thankful for all those lessons, trials, tribulations, and parental patience's. Of course, there were many fun times to our childhood adventures.

And there was more to all our adventures than learning about fishing, sports, and gardening. But as a youngster, you don't always realize that at the time.

Looking back, a Don Henley no-no, daddy probably knew I would never last long outdoors that night and possibly planned it all for some naive girlie lesson. Yet, I didn't and still don't get it. Camping, roughing it-Jesus all mighty help us.

Camping a memory provoker of time, event, ruffing it reminder that should never be left to chance. Or to lack of appreciation for pre-booking reservations at the Waldorf.

3: Don't Back Down
October 10, 2017, Op-Ed

There is a famous quip "what happens in Vegas…"

While, I don't know much about Las Vegas, I have been and it's a beautiful unique city. Lots of fun and excitement abounds in this electrifying brightly lit town.

Now, as well, I don't know anything and have never attended the 3-day Las

Vegas Highway 91 Harvest Festival. Fifteen acres of serene joyous 'open sky' a national music headlining event identified as the 'neon sleepover'.

However, recently at this festival, a Vegas Massacre occurred on October 1, 2017.

Yet, once again another event has shaped, horrifically impacted, and changed lives forever.

For this moment, news reports list the number deceased as 59. I can't even wrap my head around these staggering numbers. A psychopathic gunman just decides to open fire raining bullets into a mass horde of happy concert attendees. Hundreds and hundreds were injured. But overall, we are all injured by this attack.

Our very own Macon, Georgia native Jason Aldean was the singer on stage during the dreadful incident in Las Vegas. Families, teens, kids, concert goers just out and about for a routine nightly event of sheer pleasure. Lasers pointed right into his crowd. Rampage, brutal carnage, and terror showered down.

I remember Don Henley's statement about 'seeing a white light' out in the middle of your audience. That as a singer on stage you don't know what that's like to try to focus on singing, suddenly there a potential 'laser scope' in the crowd. Henley defined "Is it a camera or someone hunting?"

I always respect and understand when Henley asks attendees to please put their phone down and focus on the show. Aren't we there to enjoy the festivity? But yes most are addicted to the cell phone craze that has like other things in life changed us forever.

Now, will players continue to come to our stages and take risk? Obviously for musicians, our youth, our law-abiding Americans, there has to be more deviations made. So, is this what it takes to unite us again? Changes to our routines, to our peace, to their performances, their environment, our rights, safety measures for all of us and them.

I remember how proud I was of Aldean when he returned to the stage and sang Tom Petty's song "I Won't Back Down". Bless you JAldean for your bravery, your support for patriotism, outstanding talent, and your open vocal well-stated shared honesty. *

What do we do now? Are we sitting around waiting for the next event, the next horror, are we living our lives in the best but more cautious means? Who was this sick manic and why was he even in Vegas? Was he a loner? This is Vegas where, like most of the USA, we are under endless surveillance. Where are the videos?

Are second amendment rights once again going to be debated to the hilt-yes, of course but what is the right solution? In 2002, the brilliant, syndicated columnist Dr. Charles Krauthammer remarked "Conservatives thinks liberals are stupid, Liberals think conservatives are evil." Clear evidence of our divisions.

Thus, how do victims move forward? How do families recover? How do firefighters, police, security, musicians, rescuers, people on the ground shielding, protecting others, coroners, groupies, roadies, healthcare providers, school students, loved ones, the suffering, and unknown heroes come to grip with the aftermath.

How did this happen? Why?

In times of tragedy we have some many questions and as for answers.... As Americans, despite terror we move on. We mourn. No one escapes unharmed.

When law abiding Americans unite and stand together, we are one mighty force. Yet, they will not defeat us, for we are one; a bonded force that lives by the rule "we don't back down!"

*BTW, tragically, Tom Petty suffered a heart attack and passed the next day October 2, 2017.

#4: A Seagull's Young Life

Summertime is the only season we recognize during our youth. Christmas, Easter, Thanksgiving, can come and go but it's those long, slow, smoldering, lethargic days of summer that are our primary concern. The days of late sleep, no books, no classes, no teachers. Just ice cream, watermelons, bikes, skates, suntans, dune buggies, smooching, swimming, dancing to our own musical tunes of the time.

My lazy teen summer days were spent down by the beach, where my brothers, friends, and I worked. They as lifeguards and me as the self-proclaimed Goddess Queen of the man-made sandy territory compound. Jobs we adored. We believed we were the coolest, hottest, dare-devil kids around.

Each year as school's end approached, anticipation grew. Each new day bringing us closer to that thing we loved, the beach and tranquil summertime days. Long, lingering hot summer days lay ahead for our community on the grounds of 'Lake Tonya' (named for baby sister). The place where local teens were given the open opportunity and right to control our own little world.

Then, suddenly, that last day; we burst through those large double solid wooden doors of school, eagerly knowing three months of wet sun-drenched freckled, fun-seeking leisure days lay ahead.

That beach at Lake Tonya was 'our' gathering place. Our solace. Our 'great white way'; where many build sandcastle dreams that over time shifted with that white beachside sand, were left in the dust of that skating rink floor, or between the cedar siding walls of our camp house. 'Our' small piece of the world, unknown to those workaholic adult parents who rarely frequented.

Here we found our comfort, our hours of joy and played out our blissful innocence. A large wonderland spot of lapping rings of water drenched onto warm damp bleached beach sand that slide into and glistened between our barefoot toes.

In the grand scheme of and for a youthful life, this mecca was the site for our whole community to come together as one. One group of happy, carefree, teens longing for adventure, unaware of dangers, expectations only seeking endless hours of pleasure-filled entertainment.

Attempts at finding our way into indulges, contentment, and visions for tomorrow. Human development that built many strong long-lasting foundations and relationships.

Time stopped at sunset; post work detail we were free to explore our needs. Lots of festivities after work; lots of grilling, lots of kidding, lots of kegs, lots of grins, lots of skating, lots of chilling, lots of sitting around. Listening to the jukebox or a car radio turned to the seventy's music. Naturally, the greatest decade of all music eras.

Our small municipality consisted of a brat-pack gang designated as "the Seagulls". (Which BTY started out named the Buzzards but this heifer gal wouldn't allow our gang to be a flock of nasty predator bird-so I took it into my own competent hands to renamed the group; yes you can guess who was the only restless demanding control freak member).

Only a few reserved spots that rarely allowed new members. No collected fees, no wages, no initiation, no leader.

Our pledge consisted of just flying along having a blast every minute of our time, day, evening, or night. Being able to fly was the one real basic commandment. Just spreading out one's arms straight away from one's body forming a 'T' and running down the beach.

No flapping, no squawking required. Once a member always a member. A Seagull for life. Aww heaven.

digging in the sand,
happy as a clam,
as the sun goes down.
Aww, la dolce vila
(the sweet life)!

Maybe that was why I was so impacted by the Eagles band. I always blamed my Eagles addiction on Kirk and Bert; which was true, and I am grateful now but back then-hey, I was a kid I wasn't gonna be the responsible one...I was just *always* gonna be the bossy one...

Birds of like feathers. Seagulls and Eagles. Anita and Glenn. Kirk and Anita. Henley and Glenn. Brotherhood bonds for life.

Young, unpretentious kids, just like these cool solid as rock guys. Taking it easy, low-key lifestyles without real cares or grownup stressors. No thoughts or qualms about tomorrow. No mortgages, no big bills to pay, no jet lag, no traffic jams, no real worries.

Living the dream. No doubts, no fears. Not sweating the small stuff. Best times of our lives, yet we didn't realize it-back then.

But we did realize they were just like us. Relatable significate fellas that made us feel linked to them through song. Just laid-back cool kiddos.

Just trying to find the way to purpose, to meaning, to the mission. Struggling to make some lasting sparks. Enjoying the experiences, the seventies music era, and the exploration of adolescence.

In adolescent years you are captive and captivated. Caught between two worlds; suspended, not childhood or not adulthood. You struggle to transition, to weight influences, fears, relationships. Adolescence time of youth can dazzle, destroy, overcome, cope, fail; lose or win you work to find your way, your path to your destiny.

Maybe my experiences of youth really did help influence and fuel that passion for the Eagles band and my Glenn Frey craze.

Maybe, maybe not...

The Seagull Clan of Lake Tonya...forever rockers...forever young...well, at least in my sun-bleached water-washed memory.

'A' my name's Anita. 'B' his name is Butch, 'B' her name is Bert. 'C' his name is Calvin, 'C' his name is Curtis, 'C' his name is Claude. 'D' his name is Denny, 'D' his name is Doug, 'D' her name is Dawn, 'D' his name is David...

5: Three Hens And A Frey Chick!*

(For Janice, Meesha, and Nicole-those Henley Honeys)

Here we go, on the road again
Searchin' for Don Henley
Cause surely he must be
Just around the next bend.

For we need our geek on
We need to be free
We need some E music
As 4 gals we 4 be.

Three Hens and a Frey one
Music loving friends
Wayward chicks with a bond
Seeking to hear a good Henley song.

Give us some music
Get us on our feet
The thrill lives in us
So, play your drumbeat.

Now, there's the smiling silent one
Of Swedish descendent
Tiny, blonde, and quite shy
Lives far away, holds a great accent!

And one's a Brit royal
Accountable for lots
She loves the crumpet,
Beer and snappy cool pops.

Jazz, punk, or rock even
Australia's Purple Haze
As long as Bon Jovi's
In her upcoming concert maze.

That sassy Texas Sooner
From Ok-ra-hom-er
Boy would ya love her
If ya just got to know her.

Wow, all those kids-kids, mamas, Cadillac's
Music a plenty
She loves some Don Henley
But so does so many.

That only leaves the slow simple
Southern loud-mouth-redhead
Who worshipped Glenn Frey
From the lift of his head.

Well, she doesn't always know
Good words a plenty
Right fit for verse
But likes to note this or that she can quote.

We're music loving pals
Just sharing an addiction
Theirs is a dedicated passion
But sadly, mine's now an affliction!

*I have been questioned many times on this title. Our gang of Eagle concert lassies who contain three unflappable Don Henley enthusiasts and one that is a loyal Frey chick.

6: *The Change*
June 28, 2017, Op-Ed

Change continues to occur. Minute by minute, day by day. Often, we don't even realize that mild, minor shift happen. We change addresses, we change hair styles, neighbors, jobs, weather patterns, change lanes, friends, sizes, presidents, light bulbs, change change, our clocks, even baby diapers (hopefully baby). We change our mind, our approach, our attitude (hopefully for better). Ok, so you get the idea. Change is a constant.

Life never, ever stays on a balanced continuum. The good change and the not as welcome change. However, we evolve, learn, grow (again hopefully), move forward until we don't. That's the inevitable final change.

We have to learn to deal with the change, like them or not. Some we hold a bit of control but many we do not.

Change often feels like a sudden storm that develops. We all hope that storm is brief, causes no or only minor damage, moves on rapidly. But sometimes, storms are devastating creatures, with long-lasting affects.

A few things for me personally that have not changed are my need and thankfulness for family, a handful of supportive understanding patient friends, the fulfilling enjoyment of a really good book, painting or drawing, and my undying eternal love of the band Eagles.

A vital poignant exciting, welcomed joy of teen-hood. Those Eagles were my rock and my rock and roll dream in youth (oh gosh and kinda still). I was so enamored, engrossed in the music and those boys of country rock. I did not want: *Eagles change.*

Why would you change perfection? I think overall, we would have liked for the four originals to have been a mainstay. They had other ideas. We had to learn to deal with their decision.

Change, why would they change, they had it all? The early eighties breakup broke my heart. Boy, that was one tough change. I never thought it would be resolved.

Being a huge scrapbooker, then, today, and yesterday so many clippings I have from that painful fourteen-year hiatus were quite bitter. Yet, they each went forward and found themselves, had time for their own ideas and personal evolution. I try to think now of just their positives.

But it was wonderful when Armageddon arrived and froze hell over! New change.

And, we did have to accept new change as well humbly toward Classic Eagles and Classic Coke. The classic storms of change...I absolutely did not want Eagles to ever change. Look how many times they changed change.

Sometimes, as per Elton's "Sacrifice", 'it's no sacrifice'. New can come with all things.

Parenthetically, the first time I met Henley face to face someone stated that the song "My Thanksgiving" had *changed her life* and her whole outlook of life when she heard it during a difficult time. He uncharacteristically interrupted her and proclaimed "no, *you* changed your life" and that the inspiration for his song came from gratitude. That with age you come to look at the glass as half-full. Well, of course he would; he's an optimist!

As well, Henley describe how he was "extremely fortunate" to meet Glenn (Jackson Browne and good English teachers). Especially because Glenn and Jackson taught and made him into a songwriter. (Would it have been wrong for me to stand up, repeat his words and say no, you changed your life, you made yourself into a songwriter-yes, yikes never!)

Another time, I hear Henley explain he didn't believe in fate (and we know **Don Henley is always right**).

In opposing contrast, I am a firm believer in fate (destiny, luck, fortune, chance) and its effect. My perspective and roots of fate is that while 'you make your own choices' there's a reason everything happens. Sometimes things happen just to make one stronger, tear one down, help one up, sometimes it just benefits your ability to breathe calmly through the movement.

For this purpose, I hold the belief Glenn Frey came into Henley's life for a reason. I hold the belief Glenn Frey came into my life for a reason. And, he certainly changed both our lives, mine, and Don Henley's.

So, maybe I'm using the wrong word. *Don Henley I are Not.* Maybe I should communicate that Glenn came into mine to impact. All the same, whatever wording is needed, those Eagles really effected (and absolutely changed) my life in many means and were an immense part of 'my thanksgiving'.

Other less important alternating elements of life stays in ongoing reformats and for that we can be flexible, understanding and accept those impactful changes; eventually and sometimes gratefully.

Someone commented recently 'everything surrounding you is temporary...'

Change, therefore, the one thing we can't run away from or avoid, the changes. New change can bring more acceptable understanding for all things.

Change; it's just a constant in our universe.

7: *The Josey Christian Academy "F" girl (and/or The Comma Queen)*
May 14, 2014/High School Reunion

Recently, I attended only my second-high school reunion after many, many decades, and reunions (during past times I lived out of and far away from my home state). I allude school because it was a small private school. The reunion includes all the K to 12 students, teachers, parents, board members, anyone affiliated with our school attends that would like to come join. For a brief history, this school was started from a Baptist church member of Josey Estates, who donated the land the building was built upon.

Now, I had a teacher Ms. Herrington (not her name now but to me always will be Ms. H) who taught me many classes in high school. Subjects like Literature, Shorthand, Drama, Ceramics, Typing etc....as well was my upper grade home room teacher. I am certain that I am the student that turned her hair grey.... probably that anxiety of me attending the reunion.

Three years ago, in 2009 I attend my first school reunion and we had one super weekend and one great time. I was so excited to see classmates and school chums that I had not seen in years and years. The students that handle this event work like mad to get it all together, so we are grateful and blessed for Karen, Sidney, Anthony, Lynn and all the ones that work tirelessly to continue this tradition.

BTW, Ms. Herrington loved Elvis the way I loved Glenn Frey and the 'Eagles'. She saw him in Macon Georgia just a few weeks before he passed. A patron music fan behind her happened to be lucky and collected one of his scarfs that he would often toss in the audience. I loved hearing her tell the story of her Elvis hooray experience and her articulated excitement of the concert and her music man. She was a brilliant, very serious structured teacher and a calm individual, but it was thrilling to watch and listen to her expressions and words of Elvis and her enthusiasm of this event.

Well, with my classmates, I always must retell the story of Ms. H giving me the "F" grade...her words are you get the grade you deserve girl! Yeah...

Ms. Herrington was my typing I and II teacher. She did not appreciate that I could not type without looking at my hands. She was determined that I had to stop this habit. Well, I tried, honestly (but I was always slightly lazy). She gave me many, many chances. She kept telling me that I had to look at my work and type. Well, how............

One day we walked into the typing room and I sat down and exclaimed "oh my lord we've been vandalized; someone had damaged our typewriters". In looking around the room all the other typewriters looked fine...

Let me elaborate on the story of my typewriter exclusive to the best of my memory. Ms. Herrington had gone to the football locker room and got a roll of cloth tape from our Coach Barney Hester, stayed after school, cut tiny squares of tape, and placed over my typing keys.

Hah, what a great lesson she was giving me. However, like my Glenn Frey addiction I could not break the habit of looking down. Finally, she was at her breaking point and let me have a big ole failing grade...

Now, I realize how she was trying so hard to help me overcome and improve.

I took that report card home and held it up to the sky and repeated as God is my witness, as God and Scarlett O'Hara are my witnesses, I stand on this solid red Georgia clay dirt and swear never again, never again will my GPA look like this...

What Ms. H did not know was that as a young teen, I had worked for a couple that had several businesses. I worked in different areas for them for years during high school. One day I may be baby-sitting, the next working their man-made beach-lake ordering materials, making employees schedules, the following day secretary in the construction office etc. During this time, the company worked with various powerful departments, organizations, facilities, and held business dealings as well in Helen Georgia and beyond. I learn much as a young kid, always complaining and defensive. I am sure instead of being excited I was learning so much to prepare me well for my future, a future that I never anticipated or appreciated the value those unique opportunities would benefit.

For illustration, one day my boss walked in the office and said "Anita, you need to be sure you are doing things correctly. You have to do a better job with typing." Typing what? She handed me this long orange typing book and said, "you have four days to learn how you need to correctly type this envelope for a contact, it cannot have any errors."

So, between her patience and probably just giving up on me and doing it herself, I tried and tried for days to teach myself to type. During this time, I sweated, whined, and worried so that I constantly looked down at those hands, no mistakes. No mistakes, I keep repeating over and over to myself.

Boy, that took a lot of boxes of envelopes…well enough; you get the point. I really messed myself up trying to learn something too fast, too reckless, and too hardhead to make change when constructive encouragement was provided. My boss, dear brilliant Ms. Bert, was an outstanding saint who believed in and supported me in any project or attempt that I ever tried to accomplish. Another lesson learning angel from my past.

To this date, this bad report card that as Ms. H was right, I deserved, remains in one of my high school scrapbooks. It was my solid reminder and seal for my vow of never again, never again. Of course, later in life I made mistakes and failed at many other times and other means or adventures.

Overall, Ms. Herrington (& Ms. B) would be shocked at how their lessons lived with me through many, many, many years of colleges, many degrees, and many sleepless nights studying my brain out for an exam…

Well, after twelfth grade I am confident Ms. Herrington was thrilled to be rid of me, the "F" gal. * The only student *surely* that ever got a fail from a Josey Academy teacher. Surely!

But it gets better. When I decided to start college, one of my earliest classes was English. Of course, I was going to school to be a nurse, so in college what do you do to be a nurse (or anything else) you write papers. Write papers, what! OMG, no…then you 'type' papers!

After my first English assignment, I called Ms. Herrington in a panic. I could hear the fear rising in 'her' voice. I was so anxious; I proclaimed "Ms. H, I have written this assignment, but I have to bring it to you for you to proof, correct, and make sure it's not going to be a disaster. Please, please help."

I am sure as she was rolling her eyeballs and thinking "God I thought I was done with this fruitcake…" cautiously she said ok come on over. So I rushed! Her daughter sitting at the kitchen table was a very young kiddo. She turned to Alane and handed her the paper and said you grade it first.

Ms. H looked at me and said, "she is really good with English". Whew, thank goodness she even answered the door. I don't remember the topic or what was written, the length, or much of anything except the paper read something along the lines of for example:

Ms. Herrington, will, you, comma, please, comma, comma, please, review, comma, this, paper…Ok, you, comma, get the comma picture point. The grade was fine I don't remember what happened, but I know she helped me and still would today…I never see her I don't remember all the good things and ways she *struggled* to try to make me a much better student.

Now, Swanna Garrett or Clyde Thigpen, never taped over my piano keys, Earl Edenfield never taped over my calculator keys, Destry Johnson never taped over my high-frequency ventilators, and they never gave me an "F"… ***But*** I bet there were probably many days they each wanted to…However, like Ms. H, they each did enjoy and listen to some really good music with me and strived to provide me great life lessons.

You know no one ever stops you in the parking lot and said "Hi, how are things? Good to see you, how's your mama and them? What was your GPA in college?" But I can assure you, Ms. Herrington would be shocked if she saw my transcripts. I know she didn't think I had it in me to even apply much less eventually pass college as a Sigma Theta Tau Master's prepared Registered Nurse...probably just had the good fortunate luck of many sympathetic teachers that felt sorry for the simple-minded ones...or were just as glad as Ms. Herrington to be done with me. Done, done, done...

Incidentally, I must remember to tell all those JCA graduates they owe Ms. H big time for typing guidance education. Look where we would all be now without skills for email, Facebook, twitter, yahoo, iPhones, Google...our lives revolve around technology and the skill to type.

Maybe I'll call her soon and see if she has better stories of other nightmare students...but I kinda doubt it...funny the things we forget so easily but, funny the things we carry with us through life and the valuable lessons some teachers teach us to apply, often without even realizing the influence they implant on our future.

Last, do I look at these hands when typing?

You better bet I do **not**! Thanks, KHW!

* (BTW, I did not steal this title from the world's greatest genius Dr. Charles Krauthammer. For a southern Christian Private educational schoolgirl, believe me, the "F" just means <u>FOLLOW</u> or better put did not Follow the Teachers Instructions. No half-Glenn Frey Detroit words in my world at that point in time! Ha, half-words, and Dr. K came into my life a little later...)

8: *Forever Robin* *

August 20, 2014, Tribute Dedication to one of the Greatest!

Robin Williams life became such a sad tale
how could one who gave the world so much
be suffering silently at home weak and pale
falling and locked into the muck and mire jail
depression bogged down in forlorn dark gray gale
a talented, shining, gifted genius who never failed
to share a hearty laugh with the universe in June
but alone in the inner sanctuary of shattered gloom
thrashed by the early mental storm clouds of August
not feeling tomorrow will change his life-book
no sunshine on the horizon
no positive promise or clear knowledge
no feel for happiness to his outlook
one of our saddest tells of all comedy tales
Robin's prevailing loss to an illness of despair
when the world just loved his laugh, play, his craft
the wild thoughts, actions, drama, dare and flare
such a dire, dire tragic loss to all others fair
his process rattled and bedazzled; gone away
when our need & longing for him still stays
but here today, thankful and blessed
that he gave us a few minutes of his almighty zest
and decades long side-splitting laugh-zones
a gentle saint whose spirit has forever flown
while our love and gratefulness for him, lives on.

*Totally by coincidence (in fact the birth of a baby) I was in LA when Robin Williams departed this life (that circle of life yet again). As a faithful fan of the great Mr. Williams, an amazingly talented unique individual who brought boundless, mindboggling energy, shared so much laughter, joy, and wonderment to this world; I am deeply saddened for him, his family, friends and the gazillion world-wide fans. My heart rips that he entered an overwhelming place so dark and blue that he lost hope the sun would arise on the morrow. Unconquerable private suffering. Dear Robin, may you be at peace; Nanoo Nanoo.

9: *DooBros*

The Doobie Brothers
were such good folk
what some amazing songs
they wrote
Listen to the Music, China Groove, Black Water
now that's no joke
my school mates' chums
Jeff and Ed were diehard dudes
they love this band and all their words
Doobie brothers shared their scene
in tarred flared ole blue jeans
music players on grass of green
girls did holler girls did scream
Dobbie brothers
drove their dreams
what a party what a roll
their records ranked up the gold
playcd by DJ's on our radios
Rock and roll on any stage
they grooved our ears
they rocked our world
We were sad when he
was ill, no Tom Johnston
of our mainstream field
McDonald changed the sound
Changed the soul
Minute by minute
Taking it to the streets
What a fool believes
was bittersweet
but in '82 for a while
they played on more
but then he left too
a solo artist he became
after a while still more guys came

even Joe Walsh
promoted the gang
billed their play
a chilling thrill
but five members are now still
a box set reset the flame
Long Train Running still a-howling
they played that tune for Jimmy Fallon
Irving Azoff's their loyal friend
for quite a spell
so to the music we still sway
of a group for San Jose
and at our Classics they did a spill
at Dodgers stadium in LA
and at Citi they shared the field
but how much longer can they stay
before like others no Doobies play?

10: Roots of My Music Appreciation

(NOTE: Now those roots are turning 89 & 85 years young)

"The purpose of life...is to be useful, to be honorable, to be compassionate, to have it make some difference that you have lived and lived well."

~ (Ralph Waldo Emerson)

Our parents, my parents gave us many unseen gifts. There were many exciting things about our family dynamics, our relationship, and our personal life that naturally they impacted.

As for their own youth and young lives, both hold bittersweet stories. One a precious valued prize. Born into betterment but shy, meek, kind, and sainted as a saint can arrive. She held the love of music in her and shared and continues to share that love in devoted means.

The other one, born of poor time, difficult hardship, and misfortune. Yet, cast into a world that gave opportunity for the brass ring of which he grabbed and clung to tight. Opportunities that changed his and our lives. As well, he held the harmony of music and they equally helped me understand the need for a world filled with the magic of 'good' jubilant music.

Both worked, loved, lived, and grew passed struggles and yearn for betterment for their own crew of kids. As parents, they mutually enriched our youth and were always present as much and as often as could be.

Yet, for them, it was not that we just learned lessons about how to live an active, exciting life BUT they took us to diverse places, shared, cared and spend time even when they had to have been exhausted after long hard days of productive, challenging, unsafe work environments and all those tasks it took to raise so many children. I know there were times they were tried but they pushed onward and through, like a champion fighter handling a kid or two (or five).

They taught us life isn't just about success, money, fame but about creating family experiences and holding family dearest and above all, inside close to the core of your heart. They gave and continue to give us 'invaluable' riches. We had so much more than we realized.

We watched their actions in order to process and learn essential lessons of life; on how to be strong and humble (well, ok the other four kids did). They made sure none of us went forward out into the world over encumbered, helpless, and even if we clumsily stumbled on our own, they ingrained character and ethics that helped us survive and weather the storms of life.

Of course, I was the bad seed. The black-polka-dotted sheep. The wacko. The awfully horrible child. The burden. The raw nightmare.

I honestly, but now so gloomily admit it; the one no parent wants to have to contend with on any level. The aching headaches, the hardheaded stubborn child. Well, hasn't there's gotta be 'the one' in every bunch?

Ye without sin can pick up your stone.

Now, I know how they must have prayed many hours for my sins and their suffering to dissipate.

Now as always, I adore my parents more now than words can express. I hate all those times I was such an evil mess. I hope they find love to forgive me for every selfish minute and nasty word I tossed their way. I am very sad, deeply sorry, and hope that they understand and know how much I appreciate their patience's. I guess that's true for most as we ourselves age.

Aging for us all, year by year, reminds of the brevity and fragility of life. A blink is a duration; a decade then two. There are always people and things we leave behind as we move forward through each year, each decade. Our time is special and together we are able to maintain balance, tilted at times but means to straight upright when need arises.

Of the things in life that we are truly fortunate to obtain...the vital, critical, and important lessons, we remember how much the smallest entity can matter, which not to sweat, and how those who passed along their gifts made us feel.

My parents raised us to take care of others, always do your best, be kind and respectful to all, to have faith, grace, and cherish each family member. Especially as each individual segment or person makes the family puzzle tree whole (even the cracked branches!).

My family tree held musical roots that bound tight on the surface and ran deep under the ground. That's where my first love for great music developed. "Jolly playmate", "You are my sunshine", "Hush little baby", "Billy Boy", "Twinkle, twinkle", "Rock a bye baby". I suppose the similar lullabies most moms sing to infants or toddlers when they hold one close and rock.

But the thing with my mother was she was so shy and timid she would have never sung in public or around adults. How she overcome this to gain confident to play piano in church I will never understand. Despite having family that has done prolifically well in music, she still doesn't sing in public.

Her favorite singer was Marty Robbins; followed by various others such as Tammy Wynette, Dottie Rambo, Mickey Gilley, Tanya Tucker, Vince Gill, Bill/Gloria Gaither, Steve Wariner, Lorrie Morgan, Alan Jackson, Elvis, Randy Travis, Conway and Loretta.

In my school years there was a vast multitude of variety entertainment TV shows. Her favs were Mac Davis, Carol Burnett, Sonny/Cher, Donny/Marie, briefly Jim Stafford. I loved to lay in the floor and watch her watch them; one strumming on a guitar as someone tossed a few silly unrelated words, phases, or sentences that would instantly develop into a song.

Mesmerizing. It was magical eyeing this creation. This impact stuck and predisposed me toward a yearning for fashioning strange poems or crafting trivial worded essays on paper from nothingness or from just one simple word.

Now, my daddy was always playing the radio, stereo, the eight tracks, or records. More often than not, singing along right on perfect pitch. His favorite singer was Hank Williams Sr. But he also enjoyed Ray Price, Jim Reeves, Patsy Cline, Kitty Wells, Charlie Pride, Mel Tillis, Lynn Anderson, Gatlin Bros, Nat Cole, Gene Watson, Webb Pierce, Dottie West, Statler Bros, Louis Armstrong, the Hag, as well as others, many he was privileged to see or hear at the Ryman, Grand Ole Opry, or on WSM.

The only instrument I remember him playing was harmonica. He has several now but always said he purchased his first from Sears & Roebuck quoting the date and amount due to his fine-tuned photographic memory.

They held dreams for each of us kids to play, sing, and enjoy some varied type of musical instrument. Some of the kids were successful and dedicated. Some took lessons, some held the natural skill, and some could care less about the need for commitment and discipline. But we each tried our hand at times toward their musical desire, just for them, their initiative, their appeal, and their joy.

Devotion, moment to moment an inspiring, thriving family can drive your life in the right direction and nourish your tree. Above all else, as for our parents, they gave us love with no boundaries, encouragement, sacrifice, guidance, support, the delight for adventure, knowledge to fight for our beliefs and an outstanding family unit to share, be proud of and for.

As parents, they gave us unconditional acceptance, treasures, and affection. They were generous, selfless, gentle, warm, despite ups, downs, peace, disappointments, and setbacks. They were our shield, our protectors, and still remain the kindnesses parents, of any, I have ever known.

Simple words, thoughts, emotions, gratitude for their gifts doesn't seem to be enough to say thank you. How do you find the right words that state how much you appreciate all the detriments, the time, the advantages, the restless nights, the generous love of a parent?

Every day I am more grateful that you are my mother, my dad. You are my anchor, my rock, my root, the rarest gem my life has been blessed with and I am forever unable to give back the possibilities and opportunities you gave us all.

You are our foundation, our love, our glue. For that we are eternally thankful to be blessed to call you mama and daddy. Happy and many more days I hope for you both. You are the best!

11: THE UNKNOWN

The circle of change
the circles of life
the peaks and the valleys
fortune & fame
rise & they fall
they touch us all
they come & stain
they come or remain
how we survive
is how we regain.

12: Against All Odds, A Hostage Survivor Survives

May 3, 2009 Updated Guidepost Submission for Stories of Best Friends Segments

Kim Kight and I have been friend since childhood. Our lives at time have taken turns that have separated us by distances of many miles, but we still have held fast to our love, respect, support, and appreciation of each other. Upon reconnecting we always return to our old selves as if the years melted together like yesterday.

Last January 12 & 13th, Kim lived through a nightmare when she became a spousal hostage victim. After having her husband served with divorce papers earlier in the evening, Kim was held at gunpoint for hours and terrorized throughout the night. She managed to briefly escape and call 9-1-1 saving her life.

She was savagely beaten with a shotgun and 357, shot (hand and head), both arms were broken, face, hands, and teeth were crushed, and injuries were so severe, and she lost so much blood that she was not expected to survive the brutality. After a six-hour standoff with local law enforcement officers, GBI agents, SWAT team and hostage negotiators, she was tossed out on her own front porch. Being unable to get to officers, heroic heroes risked their lives under her ex's gunfire to remove her limp body from the porch, and she was airlifted to a trauma center.

Then, following four more hours of negotiations, during which time this evil maniac was damaging and destroying her home, her ex ran out shooting at our sainted deputies, at which point he was taken care of and eliminated by their bravery.

Following multiple surgeries, prolonged rehabilitation, and therapeutic healing, Kim is gaining strength, mending, and seeks to aid other struggling victims. She is disciplined toward working with organizations to create networks that empower and motivate woman.

An advocate and supporter against domestic violence she seeks to achieve safety and justice for individuals of domestic violence situations. Despite tough times and PTSD, Kim has become informed and mobilizes the general public on issues of violence through public presentations and local task forces. For instance, she has spoken openly, sharing her story with the local community at Women in Need of God's Shelter (WINGS), law enforcement forums, social platforms, and news reporters.

Her mission has evolved into shaping victim's rights, criminal justice information, support, and therapeutic healing. She praises the local sheriff, deputies, 911, two friends who cared for her for a year like she was a newborn infant, her daughter Jenna, Macon Georgia physicians who all together, by the grace of a higher power, saved her life.

She is interested in tireless promotion, awareness, and effort on behalf of spiritual health and need for support for victims of hostile actions. Her philosophy, as she states, is **"Survival; she thrives because she survived".** Her overall intent is to help ensure victims of crime are treated with the same dignity, respect, and compassion she received following her personal tragedy as well as understanding that they are not alone in their struggles to overcome emotional and physical trauma. She has always remained my rock, a warrior, and a truly faithful, devoted, dear friend.

*NOTE: Kim, my solid anchor and survivor is doing so well these days. She is a true miracle. And continues to love the music of a virtuous band, like her good man Johnny's, a bassist guitar player. Kim continues to relish and attend events with me when we can, but she's not quite as addicted to the E's as her unsophisticated complex buddy. She is a blessing and a gracious devoted sister-friend. And, like our love of Eagles music, I am grateful to and for her and for every day the joy they both have shared in a spectacular slice of my life.

13: "Rejoice"

"It is not likely that any complete life has ever been lived which was not a failure in the secret judgment of the person who lived it."
~ *(Mark Twain) Notebook writings, (1902-1903)*

As kids we have a need to never be different. We want to fit, to blend in, yet we as well yearn to be different in that we stand out. To accomplish greatness.

We are naïve, gullible. Full of hope and purpose. We think anything is possible.

We make big plans for our future-most which never materialize. Some plans some dreams get crushed, some come true.

However, in order to accomplish our 'realist' dream and goal sometimes we fail. Those failures should make us deeply value our acclimates.

It's so easy to be scared by the negative. The fear of attempt. Many times, we forget to rejoice with the fulfilled dreams. If they fail, we hold bitter regret instead of being amazed and proud of all our positive achievements. At least we gave it a shot. We made the effort.

Regrets are ok as long as you learn from their life lessons. Everything happens for a reason; every step leads to a shifting change in life. With ordeals we get respite, joy, tragedy, retreats, exits, trials, tribulation, emotions, perfect days, safe places. My hope is my 'misgivings lessons' are to view past choices as mistakes that I failed but these qualms and things we release or leave behind, championed positive new directions.

We are all blended and we stand out for our failures and successes. So, for every moment you are granted another positive minute rejoice. Sing your own song or just play along. For every determination, gain, struggle, your expansion is a valuable lesson of life.

So just rejoice.

14: THE EYES OF THE SOUL

The eyes of the soul find their happiness there, displays the joy, the sadness, the fears, the trials, temptations, the delight in the music that caresses your heart, the good and the bad, the sneaky, the mad, the cool, the calm, the confident strong.

The eyes of our soul exhibit it all, how do you know if its truths untold, deception confirmed, pleasures, laughter, or gold. The eyes of the soul tell all the tells; what's in your eye-is it heaven or hell, is it wealth or health, doubts or bold, commitment to fun, choices untold?

15: OMG, I'm Valerie Bertinelli!
March 1, 2016, Op Contributor

OMG, omg, omg. Of course, now if you knew me you would realize there is not much comparison possibility visible. But, oh Valerie, oh Anita. A bonded pair (pear?). No upbeat jazzy tune sang by Steve Winwood about me. No, I don't think this song was written for Val B but if the shoe fits...

Yet, all the same, today I came to realize, lord, I am Valerie. Clearly not fun, exciting, glamorous, sweet, gorgeous, knowledgeable, magnetic, witty, adorable, but I am Val-at heart. At least her twin mindset sister.

I would be nowhere close to that cute admirable Valerie we all know and love. I hold no draw for celebrity status, no glitzy lifestyle, absolutely no cute gene, no dazzle, and no love for the cooking. In fact, despite that expensive outside studio my kitchen is practically an arts N craft workshop-no honestly, so maybe that's minor dazzle, hooray.

Nonetheless, I really value, respect, and appreciate her written word. I have found it and lost it. You see I am finally reading her revealing book "Losing It". For more clarification, I have had her books for years but just getting to this one in the stack of one thousand books I must read before my final passage.

Now, I can hardly wait to get to the follow-up she wrote "Finding It" as the girl is a wondrous page turner (who knew!). However, by finding it currently I mean it as understanding where she is coming from emotionally and why. Oh Valerie.

She indicates in her Quickie Version self-scribe that her strengths are 'honesty and integrity' while her faults are 'insecurity, overly judgmental'. She's roughly five-four, has a need for Jenny Craig, lover of food/questions/ parentheses, read the same books for book club (mine party of one), has three brothers and is 'grateful' and 'always hungry'. Lordy, lordy I can relate, me too Val-to all the above!

Also, remember she has a past admiration for music icons..."music, high and sweet" (Steve W)...hers being ex Eddie V-Halen/Elton John mine Glen Frey/Don Henley.

Like VB, I rip myself up about everything. Most especially the scales, the yoyo pounds, and the food addition. And we both focus on all the negatives. Those are the power holder of our mental psychic creation. Many of our similarities basically end there.

Notwithstanding, I had a total melt down on page 140, paragraph three of her illuminating book as she is describing her journals, mental life minutes. Oh Valerie.

That's when it happened-my light bulb moment. My heart hurt for her, the lost it crash moment for a brief crying jag. For her, me, and all us Valerie girls. Her cries suspended out there in time lost, loud, and clear somewhere (well, kinda like Steve Winwood would sing).

This from one that is rarely a bawler. Usually about once every twenty years or so some celeb seems to cause me to pause and fall apart. In the mid 70's I was teary-eyed when Radar made that potent announcement of Lt Col Henry Blake's chopper crash into the Sea of Japan.

About twenty years after, Princess Diana died in the car crash. But that wasn't the exact time. The tears flowed when watching the funeral lineage, her sons following the flag draped gunner with that 'Mummy' card tucked into the cluster of white roses.

How could you not? The Princess that gave us a twinge of admiration for the monarchy our countrymen ran from hundreds of years ago to establish the new country across the pond.

Then, January 18th in a crashing shock, I poured a river for Glenn Frey. The tears of pain not only drip from your eyes down your face but grow from the torture that began in your heart. Jesus: Jesus wept, Jesus suffered, don't judge.

I could have cured droughts in 2016 and it's not even done! So doggone it, Valerie broke my pact with tears.

Enough 'bout crying and crashing. Back to Valerie and weight. Society has so damaged us all. Too often we are judged by the scale reflection. Fat is a nasty four-letter word. Being even slightly plump is a disgraced sin.

Weight we work on for life. A prison for many. Sentenced to a life-time battle. Hers open, public, and successful but an ongoing work in progress. Oh Valerie.

While it is wonderful to be beautiful like Val on our outside the outer is just a shell. We are all a reflection of inner cores. Of course, me being so Valerie not-ish I would think in this measure...

Well anyway, page 140 she intensely explained that her whole life is identified from her memory by her poundage. Gosh, she seemed to have no problem listing her numbers for varied occasion, like water off a duck's back. What courage!

Indeed, there was other wistful info Valerie revealed, but for some strange reason this remark was just so heavy. It was only a concise statement made about her major life moments and her weight tally that rattled. Details of her number, not her gains (maybe not a good choice for wording.)

In spite of, sadly, not her accomplishments, her successes, achievements, joys etc. but by the figure that glared up from the scale or evidence blurred back in the mirror. Oh Valerie.

Raw exposure. We all know that she was one of the JCraig promo babes and spoke-out on fat shaming. Remember this as well is the woman who in her late forty-ish timeframe showed the world her incredible flare in a bikini two piece bare. How brave!

Explicitly, I always say the eyes have it. The pain revealing element of our soul. It's there in the eyes. Hidden weight we carry internally. The suffering, joy, laughter, fear, sorrow.

Since myself being her twin age-wise, maybe I was naive, borrowing her blinders, or starstruck but I only remember Val's eyes as sparkling, twinkling. Despite the status, style, poise hiding her real pain-that's acting!

Indeed, I wanted to pick up the phone and call her...Valerie, call me, call, call, call Valerie (SWinwood). Can't resist the impulse and if ya don't know the words to Stevie's song, while yet not direct quotes, guess by now you're lost in much of these references.

And I would say, Valerie, oh dear dear V, you are so much more than pounds to us girl. (BTW dear, you handled Victoria way better than me. I would have told that cold skinny slick witch chick...& then some. Well, I don't know what and I don't wanta slander or be impolite, but you handled her with poise, not sure I could have.)

Surprisingly, who would ever have the thought, Jesus-Val a pound girl. She even calls herself 'a fatty' like Vickie basically did...Oh, Valerie.

Yikes, you are breaking my heart! We love you honey for just being Valerie. No pretentiousness just open, delightful, amazing V.

In 2006, NBC did a hidden camera investigative report on attitudes and disgusting treatment of glamorous models as themselves and then wearing fat suits in various New York locals. The treatment, exposure, and results were shockingly stunning.

We are a culture that utterly treats weight challenged individuals on a whole different level as was clearly evident from this news reports findings.

None of us hold the absolute picture-perfect life. As for Val, you just wanta hug her. Our Valerie. Our American cutie-pie. The sweetheart teen star that made it, achieved the dream.

Okay, to be perfectly honest, myself and more Valerie-like in that last paragraph, I removed the word 'big' from the last sentence; made it big. Reread. I thought, "don't go there girlie" ...wonder why I felt the need to remove that word...that's a statement we echo often...Oh Anita.

Besides, that she would have such emotional vulnerability or insecurity is shocking. And that she would share herself so boldly, so honestly, so enduring, makes her even more adorable. Oh Valerie.

And OMG, just look at her would you. What a stunner! By the way, what on earth is wrong with Valerie's mirror? Hon, you need to send your people over to the home supply store for a newer modeled mirror; yours's is clearly broken.

It's easy to forget with (some) celebrities that they are just *kinda* normal people with some regular run of the mill problems of life, right? They don't just walk off stage, go back to their dressing room, close the door and wait. For the next show, next book, next concert, next movie, next play, next stage, next appearance.

They go home to their life, luxury, hardships, and other issues. The good, the bad, the ugly, and all the rest. Money only eases so much burden, right? I wouldn't know.

President RReagan commented once, financial gain didn't really give ya happiness but that it could provide you some super classy memories. Regardless, money is a well-crafted safety net for comfort.

Sadly, for me in many, many ways, Valerie I will never be. Yet, while this Val-aspiring unassuming minded, awkward, plain-Jane, non-charming, non-cook, low-energetic, non-Hollywood, no glamorous southern gal yearns to be more Val-ish, some comparisons lives on. At least somewhere in our long-lasting mental journalist seeking state of mind.

Still strange Val and I, 'the pair', seem to share a pleasing united front for the written and verbal wordage. Probably that book club bond...you do realize it's more than all about books.

Word on the street is Valerie's now working on creating a cookbook and staying on the weight bound lifetime losing it track. That losing it chapter well-written, but the book is never done.

With weight loss you can't just close the book, run away hide from 'it' or simply for instance run out buy a new car, go to the store and grab a pair of shoes, check that item of the today to-do list. Complete, aww.

In reality, sadly, a different game with fat. Again, to repeat, as it can't be stressed enough, you are never-never done with the weight control balance war game. It plagues for life. It's akin to a swimming pool, baseball or a newborn baby, you can't take your eye off the ball/baby/cleaning guy. Maintenance for life; a whole lifetime battle, another chapter.

Day by day, one day at a time (ha, I just got that!). Never did street drugs, but I would think diet is like addictive recovery, day to day, one struggle, one more pound up or down, up and down for many.

But, best on both girlie, losing it poundage wise is the easy part...the cookbook recipes will be another interesting reveal...Yet, you, Ms. V, are our lovely loser and motivational winner.

Naturally, as she confidently transcribes with written word, 'you always have a choice' so I choose to strive to be Va-nita-ish in my upcoming mature days. More open, more gracious, more aware.

Moreover, maybe Winwood will get the message and pen some song titled Anita...but I kinda doubt he will and won't hold my breath. Which anyway would mean I couldn't be chowing down on the groceries if needing to hold breaths and that sorely would be a dire issue for a V-A wanta be.

Well, a work in progress; I think she would echo the same. Oh Valerie, oh Anita.

16: Hindsight of today: Letter to my teenage self

Dearest Aimless Neurotic,

Appreciate, value, hug and enjoy those that matter. Be quiet more. Love every sunrise. On your travel adventures take many mental and archival paper snapshots.

Don Henley is right, 'silence is truly golden', so please button it up and Listen! Don't hold onto regret and bitterness. Read, read, read.

Stop sweating the mini stuff (lordy, no of course not the doughnuts). Journal daily. Relax; acquire the technique on how to breathe. Give learning and common sense your all-it's vital. Listen more.

Be patience and polite to others, especially your parents as their day may possibly be less numbered than your own.

Study in-depth the French Metric System Conversions; you have no clue how, in a few years, those units of measure will affect your world.

Pay the extra funds for really, really good concert seats. And, oh yeah, listen, hear, enjoy the music of life.

There will be times you will fail, there will be time when you must take a leap of faith. Sometimes the parachute won't open properly; hope that was only a short leap. The leaps that flop, and there will be a million, if you survive those make you stronger and stronger. That's life. Gotta at least try, failing can be a teachable moment.

There will be mountains and success; be proud of those rarities…Learn, from both, then move on.

Dig in the soil, dig in the finger paints, dig in the beach sand, dig in the clay now before the arthritis sets in.

Don't interrupt others, that is just plain rude!

Truly relish these days. Childhood is usually your only carefree, innocent, worry-free time period. Time to just be a kid; so just be a kid.

drink in the sun,
play while you're young
kiss lots of toads
be bold or you're cold
eat-up the day
in all the right fun
pre-laugh-lined ways

And remember to be a gracious, classy proper southern delight it's essential you be quiet, quiet, quiet. May some super-duper higher power, spirit guide, the universe, and Mother Nature bless your soul and those souls you encounter in the following decades as all will need the intervention of an esteemed helper to manage your frequent stupidity moments.

You're hardheaded, so if you believe, don't allow others or the word 'no' to stop you.

Adult life is exciting but it's not always fair and it can be tough. So, wise-up buttercup; you are won't marry Thomas Sullivan Magnum. Jesus he's a TV character role and you couldn't fit into the catsuit, so padlock that mouth and 'get over it'.

Have the facelift, you are gonna need many more than Joan Rivers can afford.

Stay tenacious but be quiet more often.

Your wrong young lady. Listen that glass is *always* half-full.

Honestly, you are far to inept and uncoordinated to be a dancehall girl at Ms. Kitty's Saloon-so 'Get Over It!'

Last, you are not special so just live 'life in the fastlane', 'take it easy' and 'too the limit' and please dear God above, be quiet.

Signed: Amen & good luck child, you are gonna need it…

SECTION EIGHT: PHOTO'S FROM LIFE

"Whenever you find yourself doubting how far you can go, just remember how far you have come. Remember everything you have faced, all the battles you have won, and all the fears you have overcome."

~ (Unknown)

*Speaker box, still today, mounted near the ceiling after all these years… love that wall paneling…(photosource:anitagshepherd)

*With my esteemed BFF Kim Kight, the first friend I had day one of kindergarten that loved me unconditionally, then and even now. (used with permission photosource:kimkight)

*   *Birthday Card Donna Faye made Bulletz band signed, sing, and cup-caked me! It was a high cotton night… (photosource:anitagshepherd, 1986)*

Deborah, my sweet childhood neighbor friend and Eagles Concert Fearless Twin! (2018)

Small portion from corner of shadow box (created & property owned:anitagshepherd)

Kim (used with permission photosource:kimkight)

* 3 Hens & A Frey Chick: Janice UK, Nicole the Swiss Miss, Meesha OK, & The Frey One!
(used with permission via photosource:janicepurbrick, (2016)

That "F" Gal at her typewriter (photosource: anitagshepherd)

* Used with permission via photosource: Dad /Mother, (photographer: Kimball Studio) (1963)

*Aerial view of Manmade Lake & Roller Rink Bld @ Lake Tonya.
(photosource: Tonya Lewis/Lewis Construction archives), (1975)

*Eagles Concert Goodnight 2010: Glenn Frey (photosource:janicepurbrick)

Eagles band, 2018: VGill, Timothy, Henley, DFrey, Joe Walsh (photosource:anitagshepherd)

SECTION NINE: POETRY SYMBOLIZATIONS

"Our greatest glory is not in never failing, but in rising up every time we fail."
~ (Ralph Waldo Emerson)

1: *Alternating Rotation*

When the wind shifts
where will you be
when the tide turns
what do you see
will the sea waves
soar high in mid-July
will the calm learn
with the setting sun
what tomorrow will hold
when the day is done
what will be new old or fun
what will be gone
with the long run
who will love you
who won't return.

2: *Goodbye Hero*

Do you see you've broken our hearts
where do you fly, what do you see
and do you know
our souls for you bleed.

How could you leave us
why would you go
when there's so much need
for our music hero below.

Why would you go
and leave us to cry
we want you to stay
but your spirit soars 'bye'.

So goodbye for now
goodbye clear sky's
it rains on our world
but maybe yours is quite dry.

For the raining of tears
they come & they go
like heroes of rare
true legends below.

You wore the shield
and a 6-string you played
providing the harmony
our escape routes you paved.

Yet, we didn't get
that one last chance for goodbye
but know that your cherished
`soar on Eagle fly away, fly high, 'goodbye'.

"Turn your face to the sun and the shadows fall behind you."
~ (Unknown)

3: *Bygone existence*

I don't like today
yesterday was better
the past more thrilling,
carefree not chilling
what was yesterday
was seconds ago,
just last week,
lapsed unto a year
but a lifetime ago
with pain-free giving
you were here still
seeing, believing, humble
breathing, present, and living.

4: *JUST A REGULAR DUDE @ THE MAD DOG RANCH*

Some things about Glenn
You may not know
He wasn't always
a man on the show.

Mad Dog ranch was where he stayed
Built his dream, one home to play
Out in the snow or on the rock stand
he stayed below the radar man.

The heat was on the snowy ground
It's a *Partytown* when you're Aspen bound
A part of him belongs along
the mountain patch he sometimes called home.

No animal skulls
No Detroit strange weather
No hotel Cally
no eagle concept brothers.

To the Children's Christian fund, he gave
Some money and some honest soul
A grassroots experience that he shared
yes, he cared, made smiles turn gold.

No wise ole guys, no Miami vice
He rolled the dice for adopted kids
Of handicap how nice he stood
just a regular guy doing what he could.

5: *Brief Revisit*

Roses are red
violets are blue
I adore Glenn Frey
and you should too!

Waiting in the weed
these boys were a breeze
cool confident swagger
their lines flowed no stagger.

Singing in harmony
on the right track
fourteen-year hiatus
before they looked back.

Up on stage together
where they belonged
blended songs out of sight
girls, cars, bars, stops for the night.

Southern Cally dudes
blue jeans, cowboy boots
red brick trimmed pantsuit
voices primed yet with no flute.

Before each throng
rang Seven Bridges phenomenon
'til Henley completed Desperado's song
faithful last ending standby tune; bow, waves so long too soon.

 # 6: *Henley & Frey*

Rising to stardom
an unlikely duo
at the Troubadour bar
they start at the bottom.

Henley and Frey
what a dynamic team
with Bernie and Randy
they worked on their dream.

The spark in their eyes
the cut of the jib
the dare, that hair
what a spark, what flare.

Capturing the hearts
of an enchanted world
unstoppable beat
determination their motto.

They climbed to the top
of every inspiring chart
detailing glow, showmen in tow
boy oh boy, what a grand show!

On the radio now
or poundin' the arena
the power lives on
I hope you have seen 'em.

But now Glenn is gone
Hen and others move on
carrying the torch
and still rocking our courts.

7: *The hand of an Eagle*

What could an Eagle hand have learned or seen
drawn, reworked, reworded, gleamed
how did he make all the young teens
glow and beam, where did he learn
to pen, stroke, mend or toke
couldn't he have played
just one more major keynote
for he made such a connection to us music folk
but why did Frey so young have to float
how many more lines were there left to quote
were there songs still
needing to perform to unload
what did those hands teach to many others
whose yearning was to compost a cord or a task
are we still too old or we still too young
there's just so much more living
that needs to be done
how could this powerful journey
be nearing an end so fast
where do we turn
what's left to contemplate at the end of the day
where do we turn-does any get to stay
will we only hear eagle sounds cry loud instead
will it be our departed send reminders
to keep it peaceful to the limit
till it ends
take it easy while desperado will play overhead.

8: *The music's gift*

Every joy, every heartbreak,
every sadness, every challenge
every struggle, every delight
every light, every dark
every battle, every pleasure
every measure, every bubble
every temptation, every fumble
you can seek in music
and you will find
down in its core
thrilling enrichment
riches divine soothing treasures
like fine red wine
it taps its toes
it doesn't give up
it carries you far
it lifts you up
can you feel it
it's waiting there
to stir your burden
to easy your care
to give you peace
and calm your mind
to stir your soul
and rock your spine.

9: *In the beginning God Created...*

He grew up on the streets of Detroit
run 'round toe to toe
he saw the Beatles sing their songs
and he knew he had to go
far away to the west to make
or break it there
he met some Texas desperado fellas
Linda Ronstadt who was there
shining tender and stellar
they joined her pickup stage show
briefly mellow
and then did a stint at mickey's meekly gala
before they said
dear Linda, dear
on our own we wanta go
so, she helped them make their way
to the road
along a Jackson tune was penned and wrote
Glenn added cords and off they stroked
it was a hit and it went big
now as an opening act they had their gigs.

*Glenn's pal, friend, collaborator, and musical mentor Bob Seger had a song that communicated he could take the direction east or west-it was his decision ("Roll Me Away"). "I wanted to go West. That was where the sun was setting; it seemed to be where the party was. But I love coming to New York. I have a ball every time" (Glenn Frey). Sad, from my understanding that he passed in NY...I thought of his words that day...maybe it's wrong for me to recap and repeat...I like to think that if Glenn is somewhere reviewing his life's story book he is having a great hearty deep Glenn laugh that overall "he did good"...and that long before his soul began that final rise he got it right....it was a great life...made for the movies...made for the big screen...I think he would be sad to leave his kids and family but knows that "After hours" and above all else "as the sun faded" his "heart was singing" for he truly got "the good life".

10: *Glenn Frey Passage*

His candle flickered dim long before his legend will
his memory still burns entirely crystal bright
his spirit continues going forward in flight
his kids stand not in his shadow
but as a reflection of his strong determined light
his band performs on with soulful energetic might
stressing his driven zestful ambitious focused sight
solo or backing vocals always ring tight
rich creative inspiration of purposeful flight
for harmony on merit not some lonely plight
each recorded song soars like wind swept kites
jazzy rock & roll country beats flow just right
now his outlaw soul may have left earth's danger zone
yet his flame will remain a glowing fire of our nights
as his vastly adored spirit, memory, and music play on still
for his light burns eternal and never extinguishes, no never will.

11: *Letting Go*

If you don't let it go it will eat you alive.
If you don't let go you won't survive.
When there is an end there is an end.
When it comes to departure there must be amends.
Flying away the soul will flow.
Fly soaring to another place where we all go.
Just letting forth to say goodbye.
Just finding a way to let each turn die.
At the setting sun the light grows dark.
At the sun's arrival new days embark.
Leaving the sorrow behind in its wake.
Leaving all but the memories carry us to a new place.
To start a different pattern begin a new plan.
To rebuild our day planner without old demands.
Where to begin and how do we go.
Where do we find some peace to bestow.
Letting go has to happen to heal to mend.
Letting go and beginning over again.

12: *The Art of Good Vibrations*

Music fills the senses whole
the beat, the rhythm
warms moods and molds
shifts and changes
shades of blue
it's like a magnet
it's full of glue
it bonds to you
and sees you through
the touch reaches
into your core
the beat can
lift you off the floor
to your feet
the sound grounds
and yearns repeat
the taste, the taste
you drink it in
the smells soak
under your very skin
you pour through it,
it fills your soul
you want to hear it
till you've gone cold.

13: *A Better Place*

How can you go to a better place?
Where would that be and why would you leave?
Do you want to be free and live nearer the breeze?
Swing from gnarled ancient live oak trees?
Search for seashells on a faraway beach?
In a better place is there scared ground under your feet?
Is that where you have gone to live beyond the bounds?
Is the air fill with sunshine is the grass dark green all around?
Are there waves on your shorelines bright sandy and clean?
Do you want to stay in this better place?
Or are you going to return and give a warm smile for our face?

14: *Absence*

I wish you could stay is there not a way
why can't you still be here for another day
how can we move on how long is too long
for the ripening pain to stay constantly strong
where will you go now and why can't we be
together with you if you've found true peace
what song are you singing is your heart full of joy
ours may never mend it's been snipped and torn
I dreamt that you come back to this place to stay
and it fills up the soul until suddenly awaken
that dream is no more and we face another day
without you here on this side of solid high ground
are you in heaven or where can you be found?

*I read that Bob Wilson, one of Glenn's classmates commented "more than anything Glenn Frey was fun." Love that statement!

15: *Berklee Doctors with an "E"*

To Berklee College the Eagles did fly
To another stage for an honor high
To walk with friends
To be made doctors of a musical show
To turn the tassels to just let it go
To take their place
Among the many
Who made the music
That flowed so plenty
The four of them shone in the sun
On the stage they took a glide
On the stage they stood with pride
For their music was as well
Our own true compass and our guide
It leads them there, among the masses
On a stage their degree was given
Glenn's smile true bright no aviator shades
I wonder if house calls Dr Glenn would make?

16: *Only Yesterday*

It seemed it happened yesterday
the distance, time they march in place
another time, another means
to move forward or change the scene
it only seems like yesterday
a simple look and I was hooked
from the stool, from his stage
Glenn Frey sat and ruled my days.

17: *Deceased Decree*

Ripped apart piece by piece
that what's your leaving
did to my heart
torn asunder broken cart
tossed aside with your depart.

Please come back is what I yell
come home for here to dwell
oh please stay here down below
don't leave us not
to forever go.

My soul bleeds and my spirit cries
we mourn for you and cobalt skies
just stay below
just longer still
but your gone away against our will.

We plead and beg to find some grace
and spare our souls this bad embrace
can't you stay or do you wanta go
away from us
and your home below.

Ripped into pieces
rips that smart
damaged so our beating heart
torn asunder broken apart
clearly injured with your depart.

That pain inside soaks and glides
cuts so deep to my feet
and in the night I cannot sleep
my world is cold a void so bold
those scars run clean through my soul.

 # 18: *Burning GF Questions*
November 6, 2017
Anita G Shepherd

How do we party without Glenn Frey
how do we do it how do we try
we carry those memories
like they're chocolate cream pie
how can we go forward
why can't we ask why
are there more days of sorrow
is Glenn's in our sky
does he fly with cool guys
are their fans mourning worldwide
can he still sing about rides
should I actually take more pride
than to be smitten for Teen Frey
Teen King, the Emergencies,
Saltines or Small Frey
we will never forget him
we can only gently sigh
as now it's our turn to find
the means for peaceful goodbye
wipe the tears from your chin
dry up your eyes no need to pine
or stay home alone and cry
our Eagle may be gone

yet he will forever soar high.

As for each honoring Glenn's Birth date of November 6th: Captain John
Woodlief proclaimed, that on an anniversary date the day *"...shall be yearly
and perpetually kept holy as a day of thanksgiving..."* (Honoring Jamestown
VA, December 4, 1619).

 # 19: *Glenn & Jack*

Flying alone Glenn struck the charts
Scaling up the hits top forty smart
He and Tempchin on the mark
Stroked the flaming pit shrewd
They got along just those two.

They were a pair
They wrote their song
They played some flare
No note was wrong
Each beat was strong.

A little soothe
A lot of jazz
A ballad smooth
Their smiles just beamed
Styling words was good was clean.

'1 and 2' was the theme
They love the songs
They loved their dream
Peaceful and easy was the scene
Two cool dudes one cool team.

* Hope people recognize how influential and well Glenn and Jack Tempchin seemed to work and write together. They wrote tons of music…. good, good music. I know they penned diverse songs, snappy, hip, but some with a flair for pain that still had a jazzy heat. *Partytown, Love in 21ˢᵗ Century, Smugglers Blues, Allnighter, True Love, Already Gone, PEF, Living right, Better in USA, You belong to the City*, etc…you can goggle them or check your CD's. (Some, just plain blue and unthinkable-for instance *"Girl from Yesterday"*-totally smitten…but I **never** could listen to the saddest song ever "*It's your world now*"-yet I know folk love it, then & now).

I've heard many songwriters discuss the method they use for crafting song(s). Often, stating there is no certain mean for them, they take it as they can get it. I guess as writers that's the important thing **You** take what you're suddenly given and grateful that you have words and not a scribbled clutter, jumbled mess, or worse a blank page.

Some create melody but many songwriters that I prefer and follow state the words inspired, then the music, beat, track is created that is appropriate for the lyrics etc. I've listened to comments by Bret Michaels, Henley, Jack, Glenn, Seger (others as well) say many times their songs were varied but some came from hurt and sorrow because it's a method for therapeutic expression.

That it was easier sometimes to write about the adversities of life. As Michaels said, that is why he thinks fans react to the song "Every Rose Has It's Thorns" because it was a true experience. He wrote it he said in a laundromat and that fans could feel his sincerity, his ache, his honesty and connected to his words.

Now, not that I be '*a wroter*' or '*a Henley*', but noticed for months after Glenn passed it seemed all I wrote was from and about deep sadness. So, to speak, we all float down life in a boat, some are Yachts, some are dinghies, yet we share similar experiences. Therefore, maybe that forlorn writing was one of my therapeutic ways of dealing the tragedy of a real-life event.

 # 20: *Glenn's Gone Solo*

A part of your memories is chained to the mind
A part of your world it will always find
With a band along or as a solo kind
You sing for us with a voice so divine
Your tunes are a pleasure
A rare distinctive measure
That powerful range of your
Rock and roll country flows
From your inner core
Leaves us yearning and screaming
For more and more
Give us a tune Glenn
Give us a crisp song
Sing it slow and long
Or sing it so strong
A showman for the ages
You keep us rolling along
On and thru all of your stages
Just give us more fabulous
Songs for our phases.

 # 21: *Time*

Time heals well that's a lie
Time stands still but why of why
Time moves onward but you cry
Time moves by quick as you mourn and sigh
Time is never to again be sane
Time is stopped yet it's in our veins
Time flows by a river stream
Time flows on quick as a dream.

 # 22: Appreciation

From the day you caught my eye
electricity appeared to fly.
Self-assured and full of pride
you took me on a thrilling ride.

Winning the lottery, catching first prize,
this way I feel, I wonder why...
Earth shattering, the victory's won,
then we relish the setting sun.

Once through this
vast world I roamed
but like ET, through your music
I've found a home.

23: *Glenn left at 67*

only 67 short springs
just 67 brief summers
then you weren't here
but you were gone
flew away to your new home
in the sky or in a tree
where will our Eagle
set soaring free
now the robin's song
is a sad tweet
the mockingbirds cry
aren't so dry
no eager roses bloom in June
no strong fragrance
no sweet perfume
they miss you too
and they are blue
while you may not
be in our view
our hearts still ache
and adore you true
yet fly away if you may
where days aren't gray
and painless plays
a nice long song
that soothes your soul
or lights your way
never breaks our bond
and keeps you strong.

24: *Feed Our Cure!*

When we hear you touch those guitar strings
the thrill is real, no other person will ever steal
the music that you make us feel
no matter what problems we may endure
your music always feeds our cure
yes dear Glenn I'm absolutely sure
that someday we will meet
when you get fans together to their feet.
just you wait and you will see
that your great music is our key
for true musicians like you and yours
are hard to find
we may have explored other kind
but former types we leave behind
when I see you on that stage
and you look out at me
it is easy
for all to see that you
and that sound was meant to be
no one can ever take away
those rift chords for your fans
deep in our courage
that music's bound into our blood
gives us strength, rules us bold
feeds our cure, beats through our soul.

25: *Could have been...*

What would have been if Glenn were still here
would he be on a golf course or drinking a beer
would he be touring with the band on some grandstand
would he be flying solo with Deacon in tow
would he be driving down the highway
well we all wanta but we just don't know.

What would he be, what could he see
in his front or rear-view window
he still would be, cool as the breeze
rolling along singing a song
thinking of creating another *Allnighter*
or humming a few bars of *Saturday Night*-a.

26: *Glenn was a Solo/Family Man as Well...*

Solo sound was solid, strong,
deep moving powerful bond
he could roar or he could soothe,
he could stroke or he could jive
he keeps the music free flowing high.

He ventured out on his own
to find a way, moving his songs
he liked some soul he loved the blues
he made some tunes he hung the moon
some of his best work may be forgotten.

But riding high he took his plunge
he made his way he had loud fun
the fitness craze was the rage
he met some girl
and their fate was played.

Now she's the one by his side
sharing his world his kids his home
watching and waiting for what's in store
for all his fans and for his girl and boys
she more than an Eagles, she's the love he adores.

27: *Our hearts*

What am I supposed to do now with this sad broken heart,
how does it mend, how can it start,
where did you go, would you come back down
if you were allowed, would you return or still go,
flying away far from our sky, do you soar on forever
sailing the sea, or do you wanta come home
and return back to be, here below or stay far away
what's in your heart, and is it also broken and gray…

28: *Silence*

Silence isn't golden as Henley said
You're not here, you're not there
Unspeakable silence
Unspeakable sound
The silence screams
Is this just a dream?
Or, a nightmare scheme
Wake me up
Please be a dream
The soundless air is deafening
The atmosphere a sonic boom
No music our Frey plays
No words to behold
He is not here
And we are so cold
The sassy, non-shy one
The one of so bold
How can we hear silence
When silence's not gold.

29: *Missing daddy Glenn (Or an empty chair)*

An empty chair cause dad's not there
an empty space that fills his place
we all just stare but no one's there
there is no peace just memories sweet.

He's gone away to another place
another time a new dwelling space
his spirits free but ours will long
to hear his words sing one last songs.

No other gives his dear embrace
none stirs our heart ties our shoelace
no fishing pole no learning tool
he's gone away but his lessons stay.

What will we do how do we stand
to be alone without the leading man
our soul mourns long our soul cries deep
no dad is here so his loved ones' weep.

30: *Rock 'n' Roll Will Never Forget*

One shook us down with the fire inside,
Many played the partytown
with fire lake alive
at nine tonight
One took a 55 ole ride
down a dark desert highway
one was a stranger of the town,
one went all the way to LA
As the other stayed in Motor city
Like a rock those two didn't need a next time
Standing arrow straight they got it right
For their Michigan guys that need no pity
They both banded and they both solo-ed
and knew it when
Glenn roared out, against the wind
and Bob stayed in carving the same game
with his ole time rock 'n' roll,
right on into those Hollywood nights.
With more night moves and a sore back
we pray real soon Bob returns with a whack
tossing a microphone, no tunes slack
but it's a mystery, a heartache tonight
yet we knew now, and we didn't know then
with that smashing voice he rolled us away
so many more tours we long for Seger to play.

*NOTE: Bob Seger mentioned of *Glenn's Song* he wrote the words of this song from his heart as Glenn was such a powerful positive force and influence of his life. It was an outstanding openly honest dedication and tribute to one of his closest musical friends and one beautiful song. As fans we thank you Bob and appreciate your loyalty and dedication to our adoring Eagle.

31: *Ramblin' Gamblin' Dynamic Detroit Hero's*

Ramblin' Gamblin' Detroit Duets
Kids of the snow even if it was zero
Voices that bonded that railed out long
Heartache tonight couldn't go wrong
Friends that penned quite a few-O
some great outstanding thrilling duos
Bob & Glenn what a couple of dudes
they gave a staged show fast and quick
many a right tune they would pick
a bond for music content, fair, and square
they held the stars they blasted their flare
one sings with Eagles, the other blamed the moon
one rocks our world, one rolls us away
one turns the page, one girls were his rage
together they performed in much the same way
Detroit born, voice-chilling heavenly and oh so thrilling!

32: *Postcard Paradise*

California southern rock, pop, country,
rhythm, blues ballads so tough
Glenn wrote and sang
many self-assured
great words and stuff
from the heart of his heart
too deep in his soul
he penned some words
some songs unfold
that hold
deep hidden meanings
or that are mighty, strong, or cold
Classic hits Frey rocked and rolled
Classic tunes mellow, soft, or bold.

33: *The Family Tree of Fruits*

The fruit is not to fall far from that tree
but if you've got a seed, branch, or leaf
from that root would you wanta be near
would ya wanta be free, would you rather
pickup in the blowing wind and sail away
sail and travel far, far nearer the sea
would the sea be clear would the waves be calm
would there be others that would come sail along
what about your brothers, a cuz or two
what about your crazy twisty face uncle Joe
would he stay or would he come too
now the fruit from that tree can be sour or quite sweet
the branches can yield and scatter strange fruity treats
but there's all different kind and some are rather grand
yet most will just end up at the farmer's fruit stand
or out to the stage giving music fans E songs of praise
for that's the rage and the yearning power that we crave.

34: SHADES OF GREY

The instant you departed
my heart was ripped in two
one side laughed of happy days
the other cried for you.
Taking it easy
was great to do
yet missing you bring heartache
that never fades away.
Memories stay awake of flights
that we all took with you
but tears will often fall
remembering things of blue.
The moment that you left us
our world turn grey and black
one time was songs and tracks
now it's time we mourn for you.

35: *The Value of Pictures*

Moving pictures give us a share
a replay a memory
of that day there.
A contained show that we care.
And there's that one
who bared their soul.
For all to see a captured
moment a spelling bee,
dancing ballet at age three.
A dry ole creek bed stream,
a vacation holiday, a big scream,
maybe just a cedar tree.
The Eiffel tower a thing
of beautiful, a flower garden
in spring or autumn.
The big event the small ones too,
the ones we didn't
understand were few.
Video, photograph, movie film,
an emotional snapshot images
of a frozen flash in time.
At that instant was there a clue
of just how quick
simple value to command.
Moving pictures, close-up aim,
tight frame captured movement
or solid time of another.
Priceless shot cherished moment
life can tick, then in a flick,
with the kodak flash be gone forever in a snap.

*Thank God Henley allowed us to take photos recently. I always respect the members request for photos and copyright. But my mental and tactile snapshots are visional memories of and for a lifetime, priceless valuable riches.

36: *Band With No Glenn?*

Go see the band without a Glenn Frey
on no I would never do that
why would they tour
how could they come back
what would Glenn do
would he tour too
would he step aside
or keep the ride
pushed into metal
pointed north overdrive
alone or coupled up
band or party of two
massive devotions
alluring brash attitude
back to the band
major musicians
own your on
he spoke his mind
pleased with his band
that he now leaves behind
songs with an edge
conducted he spoke
singing his song
dominated our world
for his time
at which point
I thought he was mine
how would we know
and who would show
too any arena to an outdoor floor show
would the number be high
or just way down low
music pumps in our veins
we feel it rushing through

it stands by us
but what would Glenn do
write, play, sing, or tour
for our world all alone
or solo by
what would he do
how will we know
we can't pretend
for only Glenn would know
which way he would choose.

37: Will there be a Tomorrow?

What can tomorrow bring, what's in our sky
Will we be smiling, will we just sigh
What is the plan for the future's insight
Will we be happy or will we all cry.

Don't think of tomorrow don't ask why
Live for today enjoy your pie
The future's uncertain the blue birds fly
Live each moment with clear dreams for tonight.

Will there be a tomorrow, when we're lost and alone
Will tomorrow shine bright or give rain a turn
Will we all laugh will we all turn to dusk
Live for today and live it with trust.

The future for many will not come to pass
Today may end and yesterday is the past
Live each moment filled with joy and fun
Surrounded by loved ones-your loyalist ones.

38: Our Superstar King

Our tears flowed
and fell to the ground
how could our King be gone
the king with our crown
our shining superstar
whose songs were so deep
our souls cried out
can't he just be asleep
he can't be gone it's cannot be
or why is he not here
why are our hearts sore
our great one is gone
and here no more
he flew around proud
his voice it could roar
he flew into our hearts
and made us seek more
more of his time
we needed much more
we just weren't ready
for him to walk out the door
gone from us now
to another shore
how do we express
how can we tell others
while other's hearts
beat in their chest
what he meant to our souls
how his leaving depressed
dropped us to our knees
we screamed no please
bring back our king
oh dear God
dear God, please.

#39: Freedom

A caged bird
no more is bound
open door, flew out around
spirit free fears eliminated
free to explore, alleviated
extension span grows, it soars
his fine feathered wings
flap in the gentle breeze
reaching out mentally going free
his world is open
his breech he scored
he sails onward
his sails he soars.

 # 40: Once

Once upon a time, I held a shining crown
once upon a time, I wore the velvet gown
once upon a time, the world spun round & round
once upon a time, the sunshine shone around
once upon a time, my feet stood on solid ground
once upon a time, my plans were secure & sound
once upon a time, stars sparkled brightly in the sky
once upon a time, you were the apple of my eye
once upon a time, I was struck to you like glue
once upon a time, everything felt fresh & new
once upon a time, I didn't have a clue
once upon a time, before you made me blue
once upon a time, before you said a final goodbye
once upon a time, before my world fell completely down
once upon a time, when I wore a shiny crown.

 # 41: Masquerade

If we could go back to the moment
just before the storm breaks
could we change our world
could we change our fate.

In looking back where do you begin
how do you start
how could you resolve
a hole to the heart.

The hurt, the pain doesn't relent
can't wrap your head around
the sadness, the violent tragedy
your tears are your fence.

State of emergency you need to shout
your cries go unheard, the ache dark & damp
you block pain, it carries its clout
it damages no doubt.

Remorse & grief pile up high
you go through the trial,
you walk in the fire
it's never gone, you can't climb out.

You learn to mast the pain
the flames you beat out
you try to hide the suffering stain
but in your heart no calm remains.

42: The View

Do you look at life from the view
live to fight yet another day
seek to run, enjoy the sun
find means to see the sunlight renew
or just wanta live in the dark, cold damp & stark
what can you feel what speaks to your heart.

43: After

I am not the girl I used to be
I've learned to be happy
by living life free.

I go each day sunny or gray
I live out the dream
I outrun the screams.

Each morning is bright
Each bird's song a treat
Each minute is light as a gentle breeze.

Clear, dark or hazy
It just doesn't faze me
I'm living the dream without all the crazy.

44: Stoned Cold

It was a stone cold smart
that ripped my world apart
a sad time of grief that
wouldn't hold out relief
with a brief few words
my world went dark
how can you overcome
a shattered stone-cold heart.

45: Rain

Rain, rain never go away
it comes to bright all our days.

Rain bring wet drops to our sky
rain soaks in good like apple pie.

Rain cleans out or fills up holes
the water soothes and clears our souls.

Rain, rain never go away
it comes to wash our sins away.

46: Eyes wide shut, opens

I've closed my eyes for way too long
I missed your face sometimes missed your song
I don't know why I closed them tight
fear and pain now grips' my heart
I missed so much it tears apart
an inner core that lies within
I want you back here near again
so I can have my eyes wide open
and see each thing you do and say
and hold you near every night each day.

47: Time moves on

People come along
but time moves on
they touch our lives
they touch our soul
they bring us joy
they soothe like gold
they are here
yet then they're gone
time moves on
but time stands till
when you're touch
and empty still
once you were here
yet now your gone
people come & people go
that's just the way
life has to flow
we weep we mourn
our days are torn
we can be sad
or be forlorn
but that can rob us
of our own brief stay
that robs our own delay
time moves on
we do no stay
in the same state
on the same page
farther on
we move each day
cruising along
going fast away
for life is quick
like the sand
in the hourglass of man
people come & people go
that's just the demands
of living below
that's the way we have to learn
to live between the ebbs and flow.

48: Risk taker

Leap of faith: no risk, no reward
no attempts, leaves one bored
you may lose or fall on your sword
without a risk, you'll never score
without a shot, life won't soar
no risk takers yield no reward.

49: PASSAGE

No light hangs in the darkness
the clouds stir thick & dry
unlike the weeping teardrops
that fall out of the eyes.

The wind is damp & cold
the ground is wet & high
your heart may be heavy laden
your soul mourn & cry.

My soul once heavy was laden
my heart once mourned & cried
unlike the seeping raindrops
that sometimes fall down from the sky.

Weep not for me dear children
or loved ones left behind
I'm in a better place
where 'Eagles' soar & fly!

50: Overtime

Overtime memories fade
overtime memory becomes trapped or lost
age robs the mind, damages the core
overtime memory comes no more
overtime memories run out the halls
and down onto the floor
some stay near, others wander far
overtime memories hide in shades
black and white blend to grey
overtime memory fades away
overtime no memory stays.

51: Yesterday's Girl

Ever since Glenn left us
I felt lost, sad, and moaned
Many nights I stayed awake till dawn
Life had been simple and happy then
The tours were going strong
The band was playing on
The years were rolling long
We felt nothing
Could go wrong
But now I'm just yesterday's girl.

He gave us many reasons
For smiles, thrills, and twirls
Things were looking up
The blessings were in the song
We never know today
What tomorrow will send in
So, everything joy brings
For today just let it be
Cause one day when it ends
You too could be yesterday's girl.

 # 52: *Could...*

Do we learn from history
or turn blind eyes?
If we'd known then
what we know now,
could we play a better hand
at connecting the musical dots,
could we put life to the test or
could we change all the spots?

 # 53: Why?

I know it's a sin
I know it's a curse
to mess up the words
jumble the good stuff
I just can't stop
the poor words wanta flow
out of my head
without rhythm or glow
without style or graceful meaning
with only selfish lack of reasoning.

54: Life-storms Unavoidable

You have to weather the storms when they come
Some says are happy, some days are fun.
Grey sky's cast over and fall to the ground,
Misty damp dew stirs but no sound.
The storms of life come, the storms of life go
Sometimes they are heavy, sometimes you'll be low.
Some blow away quick, some hang-on for life,
But weathering the rough, makes the good days feel light.
He floats like the mist, out over the sea,
For his sea of life the sails lift no more.
Yet the crowds gather, longing, craving and roar.
Glenn Frey is gone, his pain and journey no more,
But his songs of our life will play on evermore.

55: Natural destiny

Twist of fate
what gives what makes
what's coming next
whose fate will create
what all's at stake
the road ahead
the curves the bends
how can you know
is it good or dreadful sin
what could it bring
who would fit in
where will it flow
why can't you know?

 # 56: New begin

New beginnings
getting on track
turning around
and flying
right back
new begin
another town
coming in
and finding
the ground
taking it in
tuning it up
drinking and thinking
regret or sorrow
finding your way
today or tomorrow
leave it alone
avoid the neglect
sharing your soul
what the heck.

 # 57: Saturation

There's an empty room in our mind
ready for data and messages of all kind
a space for exploring and to feel matters that's rough
a place for research to a place that's tough
soaking things in and drinking things up
that what our mind does to stay new on stuff.

58: If...

You flew away to the moon
you went afar way too soon
your words your heart your song
we miss you and that music loud
every single day
we know you'll play it very grand
in the place where you've land
but if we could wish you back
we clearly would today
and see you walk the stage
to play more tunes
to soothe our souls
in only your own way.

59: Ghost that haunt us

It doesn't matter, where I go
the ghost follow, as the wind blows
the air flows, the tides crest
the seas rides, the light shifts no less
day turns to night, then darkness hits
here or there, ghost everywhere
anywhere I go, they all still sit
some sit and stare, some are bare
they come around, town to town
they toss their brave, they flow
straight down, into my life
into my dreams, they come
to grow, they sew, they beam
they tear at, my every seam.

60: every...

everyday from the past, remember that things don't always last
everyday every hour, we hear your words we feel your laugh
everyday that you're not here, we see your shadow pass the moon
everyday we know your gone, we miss you more but you still roam
everyday since you're no more, what do we learn who's keeping score
everyday every song brings it back, yet still you're gone
everyday of the past, I remember, good things just never last.

SECTION TEN: WRAPPING IT UP
COMING TO TERMS WITH REALITY

"Sometimes when things are falling apart, they may actually be falling into place."
~ (Unknown)

"Who would attend an Eagles concert without Glenn Frey?"
April 12, 2018 Updated April 22, 2018, Concert Review

Should the Eagles band tour or be home silent and alone? Should we just all stay home and not soak in possibly the Eagles final farewell world-wide curtain tour? Could anyone on God's green earth attend an Eagles concert without Glenn Frey's presence?

Like many E fan's, I would certainly bring Glenn back *"in a New York minute"* from the great beyond if I held that power. But I am not able. I am not Sandra Bullock, or have auntie's like Sandy that hold that ability.

Pondering these thoughts, it was nearing midnight, when we walked back into the Aloft's lobby. Unable to sleep due to the prior hours adrenaline rush of seeing my Eagles band on stage for their 2018 touring concert, I did my thing and opened a blank word document and begin the keystrokes that could go on for hours. Racing content of grateful reminders...

I realized after all these midnight hours, after all these minutes, after all these decades that yes, the things in life that we later regret are of course always the ones we didn't do; obviously. I don't want to live my life in a world of 'what if's', 'someday I'll', or 'if only'. You can't go back and change decisions, steps, actions, that's unrealistic. There are no second chances at yesterday.

First to consider a few items. Once, Diane, a longtime bestie sister-girlfriend ask me if I ever wondered 'what if': *"What if you had married your first school boyfriend, what if you took a career path other than nursing, what if you hadn't moved so far away from the south?"*

No. Then, I wouldn't be me.

Now, I do cherish memories, gatherings with old friends who rehash and reshare, photo albums, scrapbooks, VCR tapes. I appreciate that despite a few regrets I still don't want to live with remorse and think of life in terms of what if…I wanted, I yearned, I dreamed for adventure, exploring, opportunity and boy did I got that and so much more. Ever turn was for a reason.

You take a chance or be haunted by guilt.

So, when the opportunity unexpected occurred to attend the Charlotte, N Carolina Eagles concert, I didn't even think about the decision but just instantly jumped on board.

Looking back at that minute, I am a bit stunned that I did and did without hesitation. No consideration taken, suddenly I was all in.

I wonder what that says about a die-hard, dedicated Frey girl...

Given that, it is a delicate subject of 'Glenn absence'. Those of us that were ordained Glenn Girls we will probably always have a tender ache in our heart and a sensitive string that pulls for GFrey.

"Glenn Frey may have sucked her in BUT did she stay cause of HenHen?" Could people be right about that...do I hang on because of Don Henley or because of some past emotion and ongoing yesterday reminder need?

I thought I had already experienced my last Glenn hooray tribute; did I need to see a current tour to pass some verifiable justification judgment? Did I need to combat some complex unquenchable curiosity observation need? Did I just wanta see the band one last time while I could?

How dare I take that risk? How do you express eagerness, anticipation, fear, hope, trepidation, unknown as one unit of ultimate mixed emotion?

But, still most crucial, how will I ever be able to accept that the last band's moments for me didn't include Glenn?

It truly wasn't a check needed on my fake non-vessel bucket list to attend any Eagles concert with no Glenn Frey to the stage spotlight.

Even so, you may wonder if the magic that light-up the platform was still there for a long-term E/Glenn fan.

Well, there I was, second row center floor, jumping and screaming, letting go. Like that immature hip 14-year-old that fell deeply into Glenn devotion the first time she saw him lift his glorious head on stage singing with the band on a "Saturday Night" and locked eyes; never for life to be the same, letting go to let go.

Honestly, more than likely, that first head lift probably supplied a look of fear in his eyeballs that I mistook for hey, your adorable southern girly we gonna be pals for a long, long time. Regardless, checks and screams did continue for many decades post lift.

Thus, one more checked off item appears on my bogus bucket.

If you don't understand fake non-bucket, it's because I swear, I don't have or believe in things like a bucket listing, New Yrs Resolutes, time travel etc. Although, I am really a merciless committed list-maker who couldn't comprehend thought without my numerous, methodical tactile lists or daily planner, I vow never to be a bucket-lister.

Besides, if I wanta do something I just do it-I don't sit around and yearn for an opportunity; if the time is right it's just right. Even if 'it' comes in an instant moment decide. Best to leap while you can. But that is my personal process.

Now, as for the Eband continuing or stopping completely, I held intense, complex, deep-rooted, mixed feelings in the early days of January; and throughout 2016 wavered. And, I have to confess there were a lot of days I snarled no Glenn, no E's.

Yet, not only to mention, besides my self-centered antagonistic reasoning, I know many, many fans need that band to solider on in some form for as long as it is possible.

It will end one day, and we will have to contend with that at the time. Then, we may only hear a sound like silence...

But for now, many love and need to hear those songs performed live on a main grandstand.

And furthermore, Glenn's son, carrying his stylish, distinctive Frey talent, being there, gives a bittersweet reminder, but definitely offers a profound measure of joy, pride, and peace.

Aside, I don't know if Glenn would agree or not, but as a fan in name only I don't consider that any E band decision *my* call (or honey I would be standing on that stage!).

Oddly, I am stunned at how many people are opposed to and express the band shouldn't proceed without Glenn just because __*they*__ don't want it too and that they know for sure Glenn wouldn't want it either.

Glenn shared after release of "After Hours" he had plans and ideas for more records and that he was continuing conversations for upcoming music. He shared "we know what we're doing...it's all about balance you know, it's, you know, the real world is calling right now."

But, unexpectedly and tragically, 'personal life' reality of the real world got in his way. Like all of us, till the end he was still making plans.

Sadly, I do not know G Frey, but there are those that are so majorly oppose to the band now and emphasize it a fact, that they know the band should be done. They know?

Guess "they" knew Glenn personally, because some express they are very angry that Henley is on stage as an Eagle and enumerate Glenn would not have wanted or liked this current situation. I'm glad they know his decisions so well.

Whereas, I don't feel if Glenn could have been opposed, Henley, Satan, Deacon or Cindy Frey would support the current E band touring team. I've deeply discussed in prior articles what an honor it is and how proud I felt Glenn would be of and for Deak, so I won't rehash.

It seems, most of Eagles, Glenn fans, Henley fans, and Doolin' Darlin' Walsh fans are ecstatic it continues (no the DD is not a typo). Many of Glenn's close friends and song writing teammates have openly voiced positives about the touring. Some even commented in 2016 the band was done; it couldn't continue without Glenn. Still, they are not the ones resonating concerns openly about band decisions, so why are fans?

Hearsay or speculation is when you pass judgement on things and situations when you weren't even there. How do you know? How do you understand?

Most of us are just outside fans, reflecting, assuming, lecturing, pondering, opining. We weren't present on the frontline.

If you are just a fan, be a fan.

Be a fan, enjoy the band, see 'em take their stand, play the stage, it's the rage, that Eagles craze, there could be ways, they all could fade, into the haze, of no more days...Well, okay let's let Henley write 'em!

And, well Henley is an Eagle.

One thing I admire about Don Henley, besides that unbeatable voice, he never gives up. The man doesn't sit on his laurels.

Of course, he is a gifted singer, and do I even need to express a dad-burn, bang-up, top-notched first-class one.

Yes, it is apparent I am quite prejudiced when it comes to the Hen and the Henley voice. In reality, Henley is the primary leading judgment-maker and van guard governor now of the band. The bell sheep. And, legally he is probably the only legit Eagles remaining member.

Some complain HenHen is too serious. As Joe Walsh and Robin Williams, two greats declared, 'so what'? Yet now, Henley seems to be really letting his guard down; to be letting go.

For me, I like that Henley seriously considers every single intimate detail. If you've ever been to anything that DHenley has touched, you know it is an out of this world unique experience. And it's expensive; but so are most concerts, cruises, vacations, amusement parks...

More important, I don't feel, as many hostilely render, that Henley does things because of financial need or gain.

Now, certainly through the decades, I, by far haven't always agreed hundred percent with all their decisions. There were times I knew for sure; the butter had slid clean clear off their biscuits.

Believe me, this rebellious gal was piercingly opposed at the time for Joe Walsh to join the band, for Glenn to cut my head of his hair, for the band to take a fourteen-year divorce. And, as well maybe not their decision but still I loudly screeched 'that is a life-size bronze statue' of who? More recently bemoaned, 'what an opening act', Holy Baby Jesus, HenHen You are the Eagles son. (Then I realized, a couple were Jimmy Buffett or Doobies, so I kinda chilled).

Well, how dare Hen not phone or drive over to my house and ask me for some advice!

But Mr. Henley seems to try to do what is best for the band. He deeply appears to love being a musician. And, lord knows he does NOT need the dough (or my expert advice).

Further, as much as I would like to, I do not know Mr. Henley either. But I do realize that he could live exceptionally well from the royalties of Hotel Cally alone and that is just one of the band's many success stories. They definitely, when it swing by, grabbed the brass ring.

Do people not realize how wealthy they are? That band took off like a rocket ship.

While many bands or singers struggle for years even decades, they were almost instantaneous hits. The Biggest selling American band of all times; of all time in history! That was just the group prosperity not even considering the many other endeavors they accomplished.

Personally, I feel that more than likely the band succeeded so well because of the songs and the connective ability they made to our own world. (And, lord it didn't hurt that Glenn Frey was sooooo easy on the eyes!)

The music beckoned us. And we came rising to its call. For most, that enthralling music continues to beckon.

Moreover, those mesmerizing masterpiece songs are the reason so many fans convey E band wrote the soundtrack to their lives. And, in no disrespect, Glenn was one that could make each individual fan feel center-point special in any environment. His interaction, connect-ability, personality were unmatched. (Partial much girlie)!

On a different chord, yes, without a doubt, it's not cheap to attend an Econcert. You should hear Henley rattle off the aspects on the tractor trailers, crew, security etc.

Coupled with that, I realize and am sadden by the fact that there are deeply loyal Efans that can't afford to attend due to costs. I hear this way too often. Maybe it is Satan's fault; is the cost comparable to other bands? Our band has many hands to feed, many ways they must divide their cash flow. There is a passel of folk just on the raised platform alone to provide the music.

Despite their vast wealthy accumulation, are they supposed to just play for us for free?

I know that there are many that won't have the choice to witness the band live but still are earnest, dedicated followers. That breaks my heart for these fans; especially because I realize what they will truly miss out on experiencing.

And some are convinced they never wanta see the band again. Understandably, that's your decision. I try to remain open-minded and am able to defend my beliefs; still some are just bitter. By this point in time, hasn't there been enough Eagles bashing?

Wasted time? We don't have the time to waste.

In the same fashion, we don't need more negative ambivalence wasted on our Eagles world. Although, Eagles have had past conflict, the band is trying to travel around and share the craving in song with and for us one more time.

For most of us, when we're gone your time flame light extinguishes. Notably, there a RTravis song that expresses out there is a darkness, yearning to take what's good and fair to waste, but that 'heroes' and 'light' are saving graces that causes darkness to turn right.

We all lost Glenn Frey.

Glenn's light can and will live in our hearts forever. If you loved Glenn Frey, we are sorry for your loss. My heart bleeds for each fan and your personal grief; I know for I am one of you. Now 'I wish you peace' and may you find some comforting mean to "get over it' and let it go.

After forty-five years as public personas, they have been through the fires, rose from the ashes, fanned the flame, and come through the combustion. Yes, maybe 'kinda bent but they (still) ain't breakin' and their light today still shines on bright.

Yet, no life escapes hardship. The band's life certainly experienced their share of public and private joys and struggles. In many ways, we hold a need to be a part of all of that, every aspect, which as musical figures has to be extremely difficult.

As well for entertainers, so much of their lives are on display for open public property discussion. It is easy to forget they are humans being with a regular life off-stage; ups, valleys, loves, battles, challenges, loss, delight.

Today, they seem to focus more on their positives.

Still, things are not always going to be peaches and bed-lined roses for any of us. I appreciate that we all at times need to utilize our first amendment and sometimes we just need to vent and/or voice our frustration.

We all have bad days and at times a bad outlook; this too shall and usually passes on rapidly. Music lovers are an extremely tolerant nation.

This band has stood the test of time and survived. There has and will always be cynics.

Once upon a time, another band cynically said the Eagles made the decision to reunite post the 'hell freezes over' period and keep touring because they were bored. Yeah right, bored.

Eband, especially Don Henley, makes decisions every day that, like one of Ellie Mae Clampett's biscuits tossed by the cement pond out in the Beverly Hills sun for three days, would crumble most of us and probably more rapidly many of his critics. If you want to still be a fan, try to let go of your distaste and focus on your granted positives while you can and before hell may actually and permanently freeze.

Bands and music are our escape and should be relished. If you don't continue to relish the music and the current revision, seek another source. Good luck with finding another Eagles band that can hold up to standard and fulfillment nowadays.

That music bonded us as strangers worldwide; we were all in this together. In a cosmos filled with dissension, that music connects fans; it was us, them, and their music against the world outside.

The band's legacy is that music. Our music from youth. The songs and those young desperado guys of the band were why we all became fans. It was and remains our gift. It's Glenn Frey, Bernie Leadon, Randy Meisner and Don Henley's inception legacy. It is Deacon Frey's heritage.

Again, overtime, for whatever reason, this beloved band will be no more, and we won't have the option for any E music live on a stage or in concert.

Markedly, a key point Irving Azoff furnished, he didn't view this concert year as "really an Eagles tour; it's really a *celebration of their music*. We just kind of do things that feel right."

After that, that become my view as well.

Maybe it is somewhat strange and different. But is it really that different? Although, never dull, the E's are usually pretty predictable in a concert stage setting. Yet still they provide and give us what we want and need, those astonishing songs of delight and fulfillment. A few hours to 'let go'; to pause in a madcap overwhelming space and just enjoy.

Maybe it is difficult to witness VGill on some stage sing Glenn's songs when you just want it to be Glenn. Glenn is not out center front and sadly cannot stand on stage with his band.

Does that mean we should not attend concerts or that the Eags should not be a band still giving us music? Is the price too expensive? Should we let go or should we just go?

Nonetheless, reunited yet again and going strong as ever, 'the heat is on'. You forget these captivating musical guys are seventy years young (why do we all keep mentioning their age).

All things considered, maybe there were some in the audience not shouting, not partying, not supporting or not enjoying the show. That said, I didn't witness or feel that was the view at Spectrum Center when those 'bored' desperados took the stage to a sold-out venue.

I was there enthralled by the revised band; Deak carving his niche, his shining presence and that smile like papa Frey's radiates. His voice subtle, gentle, soft unlike Glenn's powerful dynamic practiced pitch.

He often tilts as well, holds his head down, which was so like Glenn in the earliest days. But he's being Deacon, not trying to be dad, and we root for and completely adore him.

Many admirers comment he's cool as a cucumber and that he was daddy's ultimate departing gift to the band. Deacon Blues is quite good, full of natural impressive ability. It is obvious he loves making and playing music. When he humbly folds his hands over his heart, as he frequently does, it's so refreshing, sweet, and simply irresistible.

"You have no idea what this means to me. This is the blessing of a lifetime" D Frey said to the crowd during Eagles Des Moines Wells Fargo Arena performance.

In fact, Deacon tweeted after his July 15, 2017 first night Dodgers Stadium Eagles performance: *"Ain't nothin' but a G (lenn) thang! I was so scared man. Thank you to everyone for hangin with we through my first run with bulls."* A grand slam out of the park; that is cool cucumber class! (I'm telling y'all them Frey boys 'far-shore' know Southern tongue).

Bless him, I hope dear Deak understands what his presence on that stage means to fans. We are all richly fortunate he is accompanying our band of performers. Young Frey acknowledges the worst thing that has ever happened to his life piloted him to the E stage.

There again, I would think in some way it has to be a little rough for him that Glenn is absent. That has to be a mighty deep 'common thread' pull on his heart string.

Essentially, as for last night's 'bored' bandmates JWalsh brought the house tumbling down or actually rising up roaring when he commanded the stage.

Naturally, Joe Walsh's frolicking greased as fried lard entertainment didn't just stoke the inferno, he got the frisky flames of hell rolling higher than a bomb-fire full of brimstone. Like the sweltering sun on Scarlett's midsummer colonial plantation, Uncle Joe was 'hotter than hell and half of Georgia.' From the mainstage, a cascading force rolled outward, growing over, swept through the arena. Letting go, the embers rose, the sensation of soot hung in the air as that Walsh fire popped, sizzled, and crackled. His purely devilish heat wave leaves you wondering how the power outages don't rain you straight into darkness.

Aside from all that, well simply put, he's just basically divine intervention or just basically divine "baloney".

Next, Timmy Bruce Schmit, still mending and still needing stool prop, holds the ownership of the sweet tender quite one that is so often overlooked for his vocals, songwriting musical talent, and bass guitarist skills, which were indeed on game point.

Timothy spoke more words in Charlotte than I ever hear him say on stage as an E. It was exciting to hear him take a more active vocal role. We better injury the other foot! After "Those Shoes" I wanted Don Henley just to point to Timmy left boot-he did not.

Just FYI, March 14th Chicago 'break-A-leg' show TBS was on crutches; later progressed to left lower extremity hard-bottom ortho walking boot. Timmy said he fell in the shower the night before but that it wasn't a 'serious' injury. He said it was a "help, I've fallen and can't get up moment." Henley joked it was from a "horrible gardening accident".

Henley's reference I speculate was from the Spinal Tap movie as there were a succession of bandmates who succumbed to mysterious circumstances, including one who passed from a "horrible gardening accident". (Authorities advice to that band-don't pick at it-don't investigate.) Jean Cromie-Schmit, TBS's wife, was Ethereal Woman in "This is Spinal Tap."

Moving on, as a deep-embedded Glenn Girl, when I sat down in my seat, I still somewhat slightly hung to the fence rail with Vince, the newest force to be reckoned with. But, oh gosh the country boy or as he quantified 'new dude in town' did good.

Letting go, I soaked in all the heart-pounding moments for the charm was there. Henley commented the 12th was Vince's birthday and naturally a musical treat followed. VG of course holds outstanding harmony vocals, star power, name recognition, is an accomplished country artist. He is a better fit than I wanted to imagine and humbly appreciates being included in our band.

And then, there's Don Henley.

Can we just take a pause and say again the words: "Don Henley".

The Hen was at his finest; but when is he not. Henley remains the king of all changeups. The man knows how to take even his own works and reshape the magic into his own works.

No shaky, hoarse, flat, vacillating voice on any tune as some occasionally of recent cite. Flat voice, flat? Are my tainted presumptive deep-Henley-loving 'rose-colored' ears deceiving me? Don Henley sings flat notes? Flat notes!?!

That 'Golden Throat' yet again was a mixture of raw sweeping undiluted physics. He thoroughly enjoyed himself, smiled, laughed, and was more relaxed, more chilled than he has ever displayed on stage. Just pure inspiring grace. What more needs to be said about this incomparable human being. It's Don Henley...

It was and always is rough on my soul when Henley takes center stage to sings his beautiful partner-in-crime team-effort complied "Desperado". That yin and that yang emotional experience witnessing him hit "before it's too late".

There again, back to pulling on more heart strings. It is his closer and at that moment I had a strange sense of peace for Glenn.

It was not an 'I miss Glenn' as I expected. It was more a feeling of pride of and for Glenn. Of and for Henley and what this band, my band, our band accomplished. Suddenly, you realize, oh no the concert ends here, with Henley's thrilling final defining notes...it's over.

Then, that last bow, that final exit from the stage.

Awaiting preshow, I was thinking 'bored' Don Henley's gonna have to get up early in the morning to surpass the 'radios from the rafter's' (creativity from his last solo touring shows). Deacon Frey and dad's brothers are gonna have to put on one grand shownuff 'show and tell' for me to get off the platform 'oh my poor, poor pitiful me daddy is absence mode'.

No Glenn couldn't be there, but his presence was. His heroes, his energy, and his light was. Above all, you could feel his spirit.

> Your roots were sassy
> your spirit is free
> the answers come
> when we let them be.

That night, Henley ended Desperado, lowered his head and the lights went down. Then, as the lights returned, the guys gathered together yet again on stage. As Henley locked arms with Timmy and Deacon, each band member was patting another's back, smiling, absorbing that single moment.

In unison, following Henley's lead they bent down forward, took that bow and raised heads; I was focused on faces full of content, gratitude, satisfaction.

It had all begun, decades before, with just a single head lift and that night peace flowed through me from another Frey's broad-smiling exciting head rise.

The guys bravely, humbly waved graciously thanks, thanks, and thanks as they very slowly departed. They used to rush off stage but seemed almost hesitant to leave us as quickly.

Eventually them each, let go and walked away. Henley left first, followed by Timothy (okay limping for Timmy, but he did raise those crutches as he hopped away). Deak smiling waving, sunglasses propped just like daddy (how those Frey guys bows or bounce without losing them-guess, it's the hair…).

Then last, Uncle Joe and Vince embraced together when Vince placed his left hand on Walsh's left shoulder as they strolled from the stage floor; each musician thrilled to have been there for their fans and their fans there watching them exit, praying and screaming for another return, another encore, and another head lift.

For most of us, as earlier interject, this tour may forever be our last staged Eagles show. I understood the joy they shared and that despite all the in-between shows, yesterdays, and yesteryears, they relished their fans today just as much as we each did them, their time, their focus, their dedication, their songs. Our songs. Our band.

After the show, I realized what a rare exhilarating moment in my life this instant was. It was that eventful moment for letting go. Fortunately, I had been blessed to grow up in the seventies, experiencing the band's rise, reassured they are superstar legends, reminded this band and 'all' it's members still stand as a highly valuable Classic National Treasure.

Every performance the current band gets better and better, tighter and tighter, happier and bonded more firmly. They are just enjoying themselves, the songs, the jamming, the harmonies, the fans. Less stress, more fun, more savor, more amusement. The lights, the technical show, the backing band, the scenic scenes move and perform with flawless precision.

Now, like our dear beloved, one of a kind, Uncle Joe, Song: "Family" (By: Joe Walsh), *I too am thankful, blessed, grateful 'One Day at A Time' for all those great times and everything "good that surrounds me" too Joe.*

Grateful to journey along with their powerful music, witness to progressive change ups, share their ups, valleys, loves, battles, challenges, loss, delight...

I am not saying you should come.

If you don't want to be or can't be there, stay home, play whatever music fits your fancy, listen to the silence, move forward with you daily joy bucket list items, and may any of your darkness turn to the 'right'.

Matter of fact, Henley stresses that the "silence is good"; certainly, he would know best. In view of my inconsequential opinion he is always right, but I don't prefer the silence.

Yet, I get it and Don Henley deserves to be respected. Especially, about band decisions.

Be that as it may, as for Eagles or Henley events, I have yet to attend any that I came away disappointed. I never had a single regret. I have never complained, "man, I would sure like Satan to give me my money back."

Anyway, how many more flights for this band? One day their light will let go, flicker, and go out. That ending bow, that last encore, that final exit from the stage-dear God, I hope it's not for a long, long, long, long time.

While some says the band should have slung the steel horses over their back and walked off into the sunset; others are clearly thankful the band is still actively taking a stage.

Albeit, while I admit it is distinctly altered for a Glenn Girl, **it is still our Eagles**. Glenn and JackT wrote about never knowing what could happen tomorrow, thus for today, I, like Henley, reserve the right on occasion to choose to change my mind.

And, in reflection, I am obviously grateful that I took a risk to hold another precious memory that will last a lifetime. Did fate take me there? Luck? 'What if' I had not gone? Where would my mindset have landed? By being open-minded my current band perspective shifted.

Granted that, those that want to attend a priceless Eagles: *'celebration of their music'* after Glenn Frey will and at present can.

So, of those that attended recent concerts how many of them state "I regret" going? How many 'let go'? How many complain that I was there in the arena enjoying our band...

"Take a leap into the unknown and know that where you land,
is where you are meant to be."
~ (Unknown)

EPILOGUE

"Glenn Frey was full of determination, an immense shot of courage, creative talent, imagination and an unbeatable spirit that will continue to soar long after the Eagles nest becomes worn, cold, and empty. So, let go. Soar onward. Let go."
~ (Anita G Shepherd)

The Journey Continues

He's still here but in a different mean
He's still here in a different scene
He's still here just can't be seen
He's presence we feel, his music still sings.

He's still here as Eagles carry on
enjoying the stage, playing the songs
doing their best to live out the dream
he's still here, his son on the team.

Moving along wondering what's next
he may say "oh well, what the heck!"
As we sing along, he's still here
his presence is strong.

He's still here but in a different measure
He's still loved and you'll be hard pressed
to find better music, finer tunes
heartier harmonies, greater treasurers.

He's still here shining bright
watching over their flight
as we see the shadow glow
of the trailing flood lights.

He's still here, he's still here
He's still here, he'll never be gone.
He's still here his brothers sing on
He's still here and his spirit lives on.

"...if one advances confidently in the direction of his dreams, and endeavors to live the life...imagined, he will meet with a success unexpected..."
~ (Henry David Thoreau)

To summarize a conclusion, this accumulative writing attempt began as a way to share with others one grateful fan's perspective opinion. As well, this collective combination will stand as a tribute celebration of Glenn's life, his band, and his unselfish giving to fellow mankind.

One of the saddest parts of trying to compile these documents was that I was reminded of all the missed opportunities; as well all the articles and past materials that had been lost or misplaced along my journey days.

For instance, especially writing and aspects of Glenn's days and interactions with Bob Seger. Glenn's strong commitment to following his own path, his knack for melody and song writing, his outstanding solo career. Be it ballad or rock he held a fabulous power and range to his killer singing voice.

But I was remained also that I am forever fortunate for all I did have and gained from valuable chances, to simple documents, and remarkable joys.

On a different declaration, as for the writing, this tool serves as an expressive personal outlet device and a task that you can accomplish from most anywhere you land. All my life, I have been a poorly skilled yearning opinion noter as we usually are from earliest days.

Not just because that is one of our first childhood tasks, creating the basic ABC's into structural words, but moreover I preferred the way written words flowed on yellow legal pads as opposed to my own spoken slow-loud-syrupy-thick Southern dialect lisp that never seemed to come forward formed properly.

Speaking poorly is extremely frowned upon in the South, which of course is not a wonderful thing; but it is a wonderful thing for it makes you crave improvement. When the words spew forth from the tongue as 'they' say like a bullet, you can't pull 'em back.

But, when you create words from a blank slate; pad or computer, you can erase, ponder, spellcheck, pause, backspace, take breaks, rephase, place on extend holds, or just scratch.

To me, that's what's most satisfying about the written word.

Last notes on my notes, this process was all from my meek opinion and deeply devoted respectful words written from the heart of a true musical fan. Thus, please forgive any poor 'grammatical' errors or unintentional typographical flaws in these written documents...for yet again remember: "Don Henley I **are** clearly not!" Again, c'est la vie...

So, why begin these humble written worded pages with Glenn's conclusion? Why start a novice attempt of a complied accumulated material at the end? Because that is when the awaking of deep unrealized reaction suddenly jarred my shocked unconscious raw emotions.

And, because it was not the actual end for this bright amazing comet's presence. (Comet in Greek mean 'long-haired star'-interesting). Once you see Glenn's celestial star shine, some are changed forever.

This specular object that passes by once in a lifetime. Yet now, his glow continues.

Be that as it may, life teaches us the most valuable of lessons. The treasured worth for each instant moment granted of our short time span here in the real world of life. So, live and learn but don't put tomorrow off too long, for one day there will be no more tomorrows.

"One day they're here" the next they are not. And yellow legal pads, like so many others, will be one more thing of the past.

Glenn Frey's presence is now one more thing of the past.

Glenn's sudden untimely tragic death still just leaves me without the power of speech. Speechless (can't you tell). Powerless? It's perplexing and we mourned. When Glenn took ill during the Hell Freezes Over Tour (HFOT) we were concerned but not extremely worried that he wouldn't bounce back.

Glenn had experienced many bouts and rebounds before; weathered many trials and storms of life and health. And back then, bounce back he did. He always returned to the band and the fans. Back then...

Battlefield of Life:
To heal it, you feel it.
To mend it, you hem it.
To battle it, you fight it.
To comfort it, you touch it.
To fire it, you torch it.
To match it, you catch it.
To crush it, you smash it.
To grasp it, you clasp it.
To patch it, you cover it.
To destroy it, you eliminate it.
To burn it, you light it.
To field it, you pitch it.
To grind it, you thrash it.
To extinguish it, you douse it.
To beat it, you defeat it.
To fix it, you address it.
To love it, you share it.

Today, there remains a tiny raw emotional internal ache. Possibly due to the permanent void and the awareness there's no path for 'new' Glenn news. We long to have Glenn bounce back to us. But in reality, that will never be...we can't hold on to, cling to, or long for the past.

So, as fans, we revel and revere Glenn Frey.

We will always celebrate him especially on his date of birth and his date of passage. His blessings to our life and the E's band cannot be overstated. I encourage fans to remember that we were granted a unique privilege, to have this distinct person, this comet from afar singing songs of and for our life.

Yet, I hope he is remembered for other things as well. All the good things and contributions he provided to society not just as a musician for he was so much more.

Some of us never make such a splash. A dip. A jump. A dive or a dive? Win or Lose. Win and Lose. Will you take the risk to dive? Glenn did.

We will always love Glenn; he was a class act.

In the seeming short time he was here; he gave loyal fans just a little something extra for our world. For, Glenn Frey not only was a person who influenced my life but a massive base of many. Our world *was* a better place because of Glenn's unique courage and the incredible strength we found in his soul and his music. Hence, that is why he will hold that small guarded place in our core. And his memory, our memories will echo-at least for a while.

Of course, naturally our lives move on but it's just not and will never be quite the same. Not quite the same beat, not the same chord, not the same note, not the same stroke.

As for Glenn Frey, I am confident his legacy, his music, his strokes, and his spirit will continue to soar. Thus, one simple head lift, then a lowering head bow, push up forcefully, apply yourself, keep moving swiftly, keep your head above water, steady forward strokes. Stroke, stroke, stroke…

ACKNOWLEDGEMENTS

*"At some point we have got too tell the ego that it's okay to step
into the unidentified and dare to be different."*
~ (Unknown)

This is the section many readers may jump over but for writers it's a very important page in the process. How and where do you even start to say an enormous thank you to all the people who made this book conceivable.

Well, for me that would start with the one who are dearest to me, my family. My sister Tammy, my nieces Annie Beth & Jenna Leigh, my cousins Marty & Jason, who all contributed in various form and who means more to me than life itself. If this attempt had gone on for even a diminutive smidgen longer, I'm sure that they would have screamed, disowned, or sent me to the nearest loony-bin.

And, I would like to recognize those who provided support, encouragement, connections and grateful lost childhood memories that made this attempt possible like Kim, Sunny, Sully, Janice, Mary, Scott, Karen, JSumner, and Courtney.

Debra Bethel who 'practically' forced me to see the Glennless Eagles. You girlie are one brave, gentle, sweet-smiling soul! I am forever grateful for our unforgettable trip to Charlotte, NC in April 2018, which overall changed everything. Never knew I would be yelling for joy then instead of crying deplorable tears. Didn't even need that travel package of Kleenex in my jeans pocket that I had compulsively insisted on carrying around for days to be prepared for my pathetic emotional reaction!

Further, I am humbled for my cousin J-9 (aka Jeanine Turner) as well to my illustrator and cover designer Mandi who all provided wisdom, exceptional listening skills, access to valuable technological treasures, and respected guidance in means and methods she had no clue she was even supplying. Without them this would probably have come to an unfinished end even after it was all basically in the final stage.

To every kind fan, respectful friend; new, longstanding, or brief compadre along the journey that has crossed my path in some Eagles adventure I am deeply grateful for your similar unyielding dedication to our band. The moments of every scream, every laugh, every tear, every smile has been an element of an outstanding incomparable long run. The times we've stood in some human line, the arena floors, the downpours, the sun, the party-times, the many curves and the slides on the highway of various flights, we continued to anticipate, to sing, and to move alone to their rhythm and pace. So, remember to take it easy and stay strong desperados.

Last, to Glenn Lewis Frey and to his bandmates. Without their career and astonishing success in our music world a book would have never materialized.

To each of you of value in my life in whatever instant you unconditionally gave, I am honored for your unselfish commitment to one so self-absorbed and simple; I completely adore each of you more than life itself!

*FAIR USE CLAUSE REFERENCES & CREDIT OF OTHERS CITED SOURCES:

LEGAL DISCLAIMER: Regarding Copyright law: "Under the 'fair use' doctrine of the U. S. Copyright statute, it is permissible to use limited portions of a work including quotes, for purpose such as commentary, criticism, news reporting…There are no legal rules permitting the use of a specific number of words, a certain number of musical notes or percentage of a work…the fair use of a copyrighted work…is 'not' an infringement of copyright." (notation from website for:copyright.gov) NOTE: Writer respects & supports authors rights. Many varied attempts were made to contact Azoff Management regarding any concern or input they may hold of copyright/licensing infringement of this opinion material without any response or feedback received.

-Glenn Frey: Eagles Band, *Azoff Management Entertainment Records, (1971 to present)

-Don Henley: Eagles Band, *Azoff Management Entertainment Records, (1971 to present)

-Bernie Leadon: Eagles Band, *Azoff Management Entertainment Records, (1971 to 1975 & 2013 to 2016)

-Randy Meisner: Eagles Band, *Azoff Management Entertainment Records, (1971 to 1977)

-Joe Walsh: Eagles Band, Azoff Management Entertainment Records, (1975 to present)

-Timothy B Schmit: Eagles Band, Azoff Management Entertainment Records, (1977 to present)

-Deacon Frey: Eagles Band, Azoff Management Entertainment Records, (2017 to present)

-Vince Gill: Eagles Band, Azoff Management Entertainment Records, (2017 to present)

-Julius Caesar, Roman Emperor, (47 BC)

-Bob Seger (Robert Clark Seger, musician, singer, songwriter) Labels: Hideout, Cameo, Capitol, Palladium, (1961 to present)

-Lord Byron, British Romantic poet (1808)

-Alan Jackson, "Here in the Real World" Songwriters Mark Irwin/Alan Jackson, (Arista Records, 1990), (MCA Nashville Label, Murder on Music Row, 1999)

-Bob Seger, "Against the Wind", Songwriter Bob Seger Capital Records/ Universal Music Publishing Group (1980)

-Bob Seger, "Glenn's Song", Songwriter Bob Seger, Capitol Records Label, (2016)

-Glenn Frey & Jack Tempchin, "True Love" EAN: 0008811249724/Record Label Universal MCA, Soul Searching Album (1988)

-Bob Seger, "Roll Me Away", Songwriter Bob Seger, Hideout Records & distributors Inc. under exclusive license to Capitol Records, Universal Music Group, (1983)

-Bob Wilson/Glenn's Classmate

-Ray Charles, American singer, songwriter, composer, Labels: ABC, Atlantic, Warner Bros, Swing Time. Concord, Columbia, Flashback, (1930-2004)

-Theodore Roosevelt, "Citizenship in a Republic" Speech/Sorbonne, Paris, (April 23, 1910)

-Thomas Paine, American Author, (1776)

-Victor Hugo, French poet & novelist, (1802-1885)

-Howard Zahniser, "The Wilderness Act", National Wilderness Preservation, (1964)

-George Byrd Grinnell "The Yellowstone Protection Act (1894)

-John Muir, spread-headed National Parks, Founder "The Sierra Club", (1892)

-Kris Kristofferson, "Why Me", Songwriter Kristofferson, Monument Record Label, (1973)

-Henry Wadsworth Longfellow, American poet and educator, (1807-1882)

-Timothy's B Schmit, 'Leap of Faith' Benawen Records, (2015)

-George Bernard Shaw, Back to Methuselah Play, act I, vol. 2, p. 7, (1923)

-F Scott Fitzgerald, American Writer, (1896-1940)

-Tim Conway, "THE GOOD-BYE SKETCH/Variety, March 1978, article written by Tim Conway to Carol Burnett for their last show on CBS, (1978), also included in Tim Conway's Book "What's So Funny" page 176, Howard Books Subsidiary Rights Dept (2013) *NOTE: Entire article not included in his book.

-<u>Tom Waits, "Ol'55", Asylum Records Label, (1973)</u>

-Mark Twain, aka Samuel Langhorne Clemens, American writer, publisher, (1835-1910)

-Deb Kruger (Blogger)

-George Hamilton IV, American Musician, RCA Record Label, (1937-2014)

-Rev. Samuel F Smith, "America", (1832)

-"Forrest Gump", Movie, Paramount Network Pictures, (1994)

-Tom Petty, "I Won't Back Down", Full Moon Fever Album, MCA Label, (1989)

-Dr. Charles Krauthammer, Author & Syndicated Columnist, (July 26, 2002)

-Steve Winwood, "Valerie", Songwriters Steve Winwood & Will Jennings, Island Record Label, (1982)

-Eagles Band Labels: *Asylum records/David Geffen & Elliot Roberts 1971, replaced by and managed (around 1974 to present) Irving Azoff CEO & Chairman of Azoff Management Entertainment Records

-Jackson Browne, Asylum/Elektra/Warner Music Group Label/Publisher:

ABOUT THE AUTHOR

Roots:

I grew up in an idyllic town just south of Macon, Georgia. Hometowns are where your roots are buried, your secrets pretty open, and a part of your heart and soul remain.

"I am as happy nowhere else and in no other society and all my wishes end where I hope my days will end..." (Thomas Jefferson, of Monticello, 1809)

I moved away from that smaller town to attend college in the big city of Augusta, Georgia. This move began a path of onward motion for many years. A career in nursing took me away from Georgia and to many diverse interesting places and lands of afar. Some like to stay close to home, but for me the adventurous open road called out. I heard that calling and began a multi-decade's trek taking the joy of music, writing, and nursing down the road journeying along beside me. A deep, committed ongoing devotion to Glenn Frey, the Eagles band, and writing began at an early age. Just a storytelling opinionated minion fan with poor grammar skill set seeking to share my admiration. Despite where I traveled, the feeble task for improved writing need continued, the music played on, yellow legal pads mounted....and undaunted time *"cannot change the way"* I still feel this very date for this generous man; a man whose talents and gifts transformed and blessed my humble life.

Background of Compilation:

Opinion commentator for various opportunities; op eds, articles, newsletters, vines, creative writer, research analyst, literary artist, educator, open forums facilitator, reviewer, guest blogs, etc. This collective contribution of accumulative writings serves as an archival tribute on Eagles band, Glenn Frey, and Don Henley and stands as a celebration of their time as our unforgettable musical heroes.

"I'm not going to be sad because Glenn's left us.
I am going to be grateful that it came to be,
celebrate all the good things on my life table,
and relish wholeheartedly every valued memory."
~ (Anita G Shepherd)

THE END

Printed in Great Britain
by Amazon